Biomedical Ethics

Other Books in the History of Issues series:

THE
HISTORY
OF
ISSUES

Biomedical Ethics

Dawn Laney, Book Editor

GREENHAVEN PRESS
An imprint of Thomson Gale, a part of The Thomson Corporation

THOMSON

GALE

Detroit • New York • San Francisco • New Haven, Conn. • Waterville, Maine • London

Christine Nasso, *Publisher*
Elizabeth Des Chenes, *Managing Editor*

© 2007 Thomson Gale, a part of The Thomson Corporation.

Thomson and Star logo are trademarks and Gale and Greenhaven Press are registered trademarks used herein under license.

For more information, contact:
Greenhaven Press
27500 Drake Rd.
Farmington Hills, MI 48331-3535
Or you can visit our Internet site at http://www.gale.com

ISBN-13: 978-0-7377-2859-0
ISBN-10: 0-7377-2859-0

Library of Congress Control Number: 2006936125

Printed in the United States of America
10 9 8 7 6 5 4 3 2 1

Contents

Chapter 2: Euthanasia and Physician-Assisted Suicide

Chapter 3: Reproductive Technology and Cloning

Chapter 4: Eugenics and Genetic Engineering

Foreword

In the 1940s, at the height of the Holocaust, Jews struggled to create a nation of their own in Palestine, a region of the Middle East that at the time was controlled by Britain. The British had placed limits on Jewish immigration to Palestine, hampering efforts to provide refuge to Jews fleeing the Holocaust. In response to this and other British policies, an underground Jewish resistance group called Irgun began carrying out terrorist attacks against British targets in Palestine, including immigration, intelligence, and police offices. Most famously, the group bombed the King David Hotel in Jerusalem, the site of a British military headquarters. Although the British were warned well in advance of the attack, they failed to evacuate the building. As a result, ninety-one people were killed (including fifteen Jews) and forty-five were injured.

Early in the twentieth century, Ireland, which had long been under British rule, was split into two countries. The south, populated mostly by Catholics, eventually achieved independence and became the Republic of Ireland. Northern Ireland, mostly Protestant, remained under British control. Catholics in both the north and south opposed British control of the north, and the Irish Republican Army (IRA) sought unification of Ireland as an independent nation. In 1969, the IRA split into two factions. A new radical wing, the Provisional IRA, was created and soon undertook numerous terrorist bombings and killings throughout Northern Ireland, the Republic of Ireland, and even in England. One of its most notorious attacks was the 1974 bombing of a Birmingham, England, bar that killed nineteen people.

In the mid-1990s, an Islamic terrorist group called al Qaeda began carrying out terrorist attacks against American targets overseas. In communications to the media, the organization listed several complaints against the United States. It generally opposed all U.S. involvement and presence in the Middle East. It particularly objected to the presence of U.S. troops in Saudi Arabia, which is the home of several Islamic holy sites. And it strongly condemned the United States for supporting the nation of Israel, which it claimed was an oppressor of Muslims. In 1998 al Qaeda's leaders issued a fatwa (a religious legal statement) calling for Muslims to kill Americans. Al Qaeda acted on this order many times—most memorably on September 11, 2001, when it attacked the World Trade Center and the Pentagon, killing nearly three thousand people.

These three groups—Irgun, the Provisional IRA, and al Qaeda—have achieved varied results. Irgun's terror campaign contributed to Britain's decision to pull out of Palestine and to support the creation of Israel in 1948. The Provisional IRA's tactics kept pressure on the British, but they also alienated many would-be supporters of independence for Northern Ireland. Al Qaeda's attacks provoked a strong U.S. military response but did not lessen America's involvement in the Middle East nor weaken its support of Israel. Despite these different results, the means and goals of these groups were similar. Although they emerged in different parts of the world during different eras and in support of different causes, all three had one thing in common: They all used clandestine violence to undermine a government they deemed oppressive or illegitimate.

The destruction of oppressive governments is not the only goal of terrorism. For example, terror is also used to minimize dissent in totalitarian regimes and to promote extreme ideologies. However, throughout history the motivations of terrorists have been remarkably similar, proving the old adage that "the more things change, the more they remain the same." Arguments for and against terrorism thus boil down to the same set of universal arguments regardless of the age: Some argue that terrorism is justified to change (or, in the case of state terror, to maintain) the prevailing political order; others respond that terrorism is inhumane and unacceptable under any circumstances. These basic views transcend time and place.

Similar fundamental arguments apply to other controversial social issues. For instance, arguments over the death penalty have always featured competing views of justice. Scholars cite biblical texts to claim that a person who takes a life must forfeit his or her life, while others cite religious doctrine to support their view that only God can take a human life. These arguments have remained essentially the same throughout the centuries. Likewise, the debate over euthanasia has persisted throughout the history of Western civilization. Supporters argue that it is compassionate to end the suffering of the dying by hastening their impending death; opponents insist that it is society's duty to make the dying as comfortable as possible as death takes its natural course.

Greenhaven Press's The History of Issues series illustrates this constancy of arguments surrounding major social issues. Each volume in the series focuses on one issue—including terrorism, the death penalty, and euthanasia—and examines how the debates have both evolved and remained essentially the same over the years. Primary documents such as newspaper articles, speeches, and government reports illuminate historical developments and offer perspectives from throughout history. Secondary sources provide overviews and commentaries from a more contemporary perspective. An introduction begins each anthology and supplies essential context and background. An annotated table of contents, chronology, and index allow for easy reference, and a bibliography and list of organizations to contact point to additional sources of information on the book's topic. With these features, The History of Issues series permits readers to glimpse both the historical and contemporary dimensions of humanity's most pressing and controversial social issues.

Introduction

Biomedical ethics is both a field of inquiry concerning ethical issues in medicine and health care and a formal discipline evaluating the risks, benefits, morality, and social implications of controversial practices in medicine and science. Modern biomedical ethics incorporates the thoughts and beliefs of physicians, philosophers, and theologians in shaping the most ethical policies and guidelines in the rapidly advancing areas of medicine and research.

The most effective way to study the subject of biomedical ethics is to dig beneath the current debates on modern biomedical ethics controversies to learn about the issues from a historical perspective. This course of study is endorsed by the father of modern bioethics, Albert Jonsen, who contends in *The New Medicine and the Old Ethics*, "There is a kind of moral archeology: digging beneath current moral beliefs, values, and practices, one discovers that these are based on ancient foundations not visible to the casual observer." Beyond revealing the foundations of contemporary ethical debates, historical analysis also illuminates the relationship between medical ethics policy and a society's changing views on both ethics and medicine.

A historical context can even reveal the impact that technological advances in medical care and research have on biomedical ethics issues. As professor of religion C. Keith Boone writes in *Bad Axioms in Genetic Engineering*, "Every advance in the fulfillment of human aspirations creates problems at an entirely new level." New technologies that can prolong life, for example, lead to questions about the importance of quality of life rather than its mere extended duration. Similarly, the development of reproductive technologies that allow infertile couples to have their own biological children stimulate questions about tampering with one of the most meaningful and cherished aspects of human life.

Examining the history of ethical debates also illustrates how views have evolved as new philosophical models come into play. For example, the controversies surrounding the practice of euthanasia have changed as medicine and religion intertwined. In ancient Greek and Roman times, euthanasia was seen as "an appropriate and rational response to a wide variety of circumstances," according to Ian Dowbiggin in *A Concise History of Euthanasia*. Dowbiggin notes that the ancient sense of honor made euthanasia an accepted practice among those who were sapped by disease or those who were facing a torturous terminal illness. In the fourth century A.D, however, the rise of Christian ethics entailed a rejection of Greek and Roman principles. Euthanasia was deemed immoral under Christian doctrine because human life was a sacred gift from God. The perception of euthanasia as an immoral act persisted as the dominant view until the early twentieth century produced secular pro-euthanasia advocates who believed people suffering from physical and psychological pain should be allowed to die or be helped to die if they desired.

Although popular support for euthanasia was undermined in the 1940s as euthanasia became associated with Nazi Germany's plan to kill off undesirables to produce a "pure" Aryan race, the debate resurfaced again in the 1950s. Technological advances in medicine beginning in the 1950s allowed physicians to prolong the lives of critically ill patients with feeding tubes, ventilators, and other life-support equipment. Again, euthanasia advocates called for legalized euthanasia as a means to reduce unnecessary suffering. Peering down through the historical roots of euthanasia, then, reveals that religious mandates and technological advances have shaped the two major opposing positions in the modern debate on euthanasia. These forces have also been influential in other biomedical issues such as cloning and genetic engineering.

As the euthanasia debate exemplifies, modern bioethical issues are impacted by a variety of philosophies that range from ancient Hippocratic medical ethics standards, Christian doctrine, and legal and political concepts that include free will and notions of patients' rights. *History of Issues: Biomedical Ethics* examines the evolution of biomedical ethics as a concept through historical analysis of specific controversial issues such as euthanasia, genetic engineering, and eugenics. Looking at the opposing views on these subjects reveals that consensus on a correct ethical path is rarely reached. Instead, the values that a society holds dear often determine how medical research and practice are to be carried out at that moment in time. As time passes and beliefs and technologies change, current views on biomedical ethics debates may yield to new ways of thinking about medicine, morals, and the value of life.

The Physician's Role in Medical Ethics

Chapter Preface

The ethical path that a physician follows to address medical dilemmas and set specific courses of treatment has evolved over the course of history. Only recently has the ethical framework coalesced into a set of four basic principles: respect for autonomy, beneficence, justice, and nonmaleficence. Respect for autonomy means recognizing the right of patients to make their own medical decisions based on unbiased information provided by health-care professionals. Beneficence describes a health-care worker's moral obligation to act in the interest of others. The principle of justice emphasizes the idea that all patients in a similar situation should receive the same treatments and assume the same amount of risks. Finally, the concept of nonmaleficence dictates that physicians have an obligation not to inflict harm intentionally on their patients.

These four values have only guided medical professionals since the late 1970s. Before that time, priorities in medical ethics were determined by the cultural and social values of particular societies. In ancient Greece, Hippocrates felt that the best approach to medical treatment was for the physician to decide which treatment regimen was best based on his skill and judgment without considering his patient's input. Conversely, in the 1800s, patients had complete autonomy over their treatment based on their ability to hire and fire physicians at their pleasure. Each era of history has had different interpretations of the physician's role in medical ethics. The following chapter traces the evolution of the ethical codes to which doctors have subscribed from the days of ancient Babylon to modern times.

Ancient Codes of Medical Ethics Emphasize Rules and Personal Conduct

Robert Forbes

The history of medical ethics began with ancient attempts to balance the medical skills and monetary interests of the physician with the welfare of the patient. In the following selection, Secretary of the Medical Defence Union Robert Forbes uses ancient texts to give examples of early medical ethics. Specifically, Forbes cites selections from the Babylonian Code of 2250 B.C.E. and Hippocrates' codes of medical ethics written over 1000 years later. The Babylonian code mandated appropriate medical fees and specified punishments for inept physicians. The ancient Greeks did not establish law codes directing medical practice; instead physicians were expected to be ethically self directed. Hippocrates' code, therefore, set out a series of principles and oaths that emphasized a physician's personal responsibility for his medical conduct. Forbes goes on to explain that the early Romans returned to the concept of passing laws to regulate medical practitioners while keeping alive the sense of dignity and duty inherited from Hippocratic idealism.

Origin and evolution are commonly of great interest and importance for the full understanding of a subject, and I therefore thought it might be helpful in our present deliberations if I gave a short summary of the history of medical ethics.

The Babylonian Code

The story begins in Babylon, where in 2700 B.C. a treatise was published dealing with the regulation of the conduct of a phy-

Robert Forbes, "A History Survey of Medical Ethics," *St. Bartholomew's Hospital Journal*, 1955, pp. 282–319.

sician. The celebrated Babylonian Code by Hammurabi appeared about 2250 B.C. In this "the oldest code of laws in the world" is contained the idea of the personal responsibility of the physician, and, on the principles of the *lex talionis* [law of retribution, i.e., "an eye for an eye"], it lays down on the one hand the fees payable for certain medical and surgical services, and on the other the penalties for negligent or unsuccessful practice. Some of this "eye for an eye" legislation is very interesting in the light of present-day practice and experience.

215. If a doctor has treated a man for a severe wound with a bronze lancet, and has cured him, or has opened an abscess of a man's eye with a bronze lancet, and has cured the eye, he shall take ten shekels of silver.

216. If the patient be the son of a poor man he shall take five shekels of silver.

217. If he be a servant the master of the servant shall give two shekels of silver to the doctor.

218. If the doctor has treated a man for a severe wound with a bronze lancet and has caused the man to die, or has opened an abscess of the eye with a bronze lancet and has caused the loss of the man's eye, his hands shall be cut off.

219. If a doctor has treated the severe wound of a slave of a poor man with a bronze lancet, and has caused his death, he shall render slave for slave.

220. If he has opened his abscess with a bronze lancet, and has made him lose this eye, he shall pay money, half the price of the slave. . . .

The imposition of penalties on unsuccessful treatment must have checked to some degree the progress of medicine, and the Babylonians were not the only people to prescribe such punishments. An Egyptian physician whose patient died in an unorthodox manner—that is, in a manner which was not recognised by the governing authorities—might be sentenced to death. . . .

The Hippocratic Oath

The Greeks had no legal code like that of the Babylonians to guide the physician in the details of ethical procedure. A physician was guided solely by his desire to help suffering humanity, and his conduct was based on traditional religious teaching and national customs and on his artistic instinct. It is to a Greek that we owe the fullest concept of the responsibilities devolving upon medical practitioners. This is embodied in the famous Oath of Hippocrates, of which the following is a translation by Francis Adams of Banchory, the Deeside scholar.

I swear by Apollo the physician, and Aesculapius, and Health, and All-heal, and all the gods and goddesses, that according to my ability and judgement I will keep this oath and this stipulation: to reckon him who taught me this art equally dear to me as my parents, to share my substance with him, and relieve his necessities if required; to look upon his offspring in the same footing as my own brothers, and to teach them this art, if they shall wish to learn it, without fee or stipulation; and that by precept, lecture, and every other mode of instruction, I will impart a knowledge of the art to my own sons, and those of my teachers, and to disciples bound by a stipulation and oath according to the law of medicine, but to none others. I will follow that system of regimen which, according to my ability and judgement, I consider for the benefit of my patients, and abstain from whatever is deleterious and mischievous. I will give no deadly medicine to anyone if asked; nor suggest any such counsel; and in like manner I will not give to a woman a pessary to produce abortion. With purity and with holiness I will pass my life and practise my art. I will not cut persons labouring under the stone, but will leave this to be done by men who are practitioners of this work. Into whatever houses I enter I will go into them for the benefit of the sick, and will abstain from every voluntary act of mischief and corruption and further from the seduction of females or males, of freemen and slaves. Whatever, in connexion with my professional practice or not in connexion with it, I see or hear, in the life of men, which ought not to be spoken of abroad, I will not divulge, as reckoning that all such should be kept secret. While I continue to keep this oath unviolated, may it be granted to me to enjoy life and the practice of the art, respected by all men, in my times! But should I trespass and violate this oath may the reverse be my lot!

The oath is worthy of the highest admiration, and its spirit is still applicable to the general conduct of the medical practitioner. Many medical schools still administer the Oath to their graduands in a modified form, which omits the pagan references.

But if we are to maintain those ethical standards which are necessary for the successful pursuit of the art and practice of medicine the rules contained in the Oath require to be restated from age to age. Its chief obligations are that a practitioner should summon a consultant when he is in doubt as to the prognosis, diagnosis, or treatment of a case; that he should be reasonable in his charges or, if necessary, forgo them altogether; that he should lead a pure and moral life; that he should endeavour to be a philanthropist; that he should respect at all times his medical teachers; that he should not give, or sanction the giving of, a poison, cause or encourage abortion, use his position to debauch a patient or any member of a patient's household; that he should not divulge information about a patient; that he should not advertise in any way; and that he should not be ostentatious in dress or bearing. These simple criteria, succinctly expressed, of professional dignity and duty have been the ideals of medical ethics for nearly 2,000 years, and they constitute the foundation on which have been built up our modern codes. There has been scarcely an age in medicine in which some great leader has not under-lined and endorsed the basic principles of ethics as enunciated in the Hippocratic writings.

Hippocrates and the Art of Medicine

The father of Medicine went further than the mere enuncia-tion of a code of ethics. In that part of his writing called "The Law" he defines with great precision the requisites necessary to acquire eminence in the pursuit of the art of medicine.

Admirable as "The Law" is in its demand for high stan-dards, its application must have restricted, in some measure, the flow of medical thought and practice.

The Romans delayed the legal control of medical conduct until it became necessary to protect the public against quack-ery and the sale of proprietary medicines. Antoninus Pius (A.D. 138–161) passed an edict restricting the number of phy-sicians practising in the community, prescribing certain tests as to their character and ability, and exempting them from taxation and certain public duties. The practice of medicine thus became an honourable profession, and physicians had no longer to grovel basely before the rich. After the fall of Rome, however, a *lex talionis* was introduced. There was very little difference between quacks and responsible physicians in Graeco-Roman times because there were no academic degrees and no legal qualifications. Neither ethics nor etiquette nor any other power can suppress quackery in all its various phases. Some have suggested that it might be suppressed by a strictly applied test and the prohibition of practice by persons who have not submitted themselves for examination. There are others who hold that even the law cannot abolish the practice of quackery, since quackery is not unknown within the ranks of the registered medical profession itself.

Late Medieval Physicians Developed Strong Professional Ethics

Mary Catherine Welborn

Petrarch and other early fourteenth-century authors who wrote of the practice of medicine in their times suggested that the late Middle Ages were a dark time for medical ethics. They believed that medieval physicians were unskilled, unethical, and greedy. In the following selection, medieval historian Mary Catherine Welborn counters this notion by reviewing medieval physicians' writings about medical ethics, physician character, patient treatments, physician training, and medical fees in the fourteenth century. Welborn found that medical ethics of the late middle ages were strongly influenced by ancient medical ideals from philosophers such as Hippocrates. Welborn concludes that even though late medieval physicians did not have much medical knowledge, they did have a strong sense of medical ethics.

The medieval physician, although he lacked skill and knowledge in the art and practice of medicine, in his humanity toward his patients and his desire to do the utmost to help them, was equal to the best of our medical men today. These high ideals were held not by a few of these early doctors only but were the code of the profession. Now laws are made, usually at the instigation of the physicians themselves, and are enforced by the courts to curb as far as possible unethical practices, although many vitally important problems are still left to the judgment of the individual physician. But in the Middle Ages there were merely rules and regulations made either by physicians who passed them on to their university and private

Mary Catherine Welborn, "The Long Tradition: A Study in Fourteenth-Century Medical Deontology," *Legacies in Ethics and Medicine*. Edited by Chester R. Burns. New York: Science History Publications, 1977, pp. 204–217.

students, or by groups of doctors in universities or guilds, sometimes with and sometimes without the sanction of the city or state governments. The main sources for the ethical ideas of the ancient and medieval periods are those chapters devoted primarily to medical deontology [the study of norms of conduct for medical professions] which are so often found in the general writings of physicians and surgeons, especially in the later Middle Ages.

By examining some of the principal works of representative doctors of the fourteenth century, we can come to certain definite conclusions concerning the rise and development of contemporary medical ethics and, what is more precious, to a better understanding of the fourteenth-century doctor, who has been so reviled by famous writers like Petrarch and by other humanists. The deontological chapters reveal the true nature of the physician and show us the real man—a vital, intelligent human being who, despite his woeful lack of scientific knowledge, in many cases was honestly trying to do his best both for the sake of humanity and for the love of his art. It is true that many quacks and charlatans existed in that century, as well as in our own, who neither preached nor practiced in an ethical manner, but we have no right to condemn in a wholesale way, as did Petrarch, all doctors on account of the errors of some of their profession. Modern critics have been too prone to ignore these ethical sections of the medical works and to spend all their time criticizing the information, or lack of it, displayed in other parts of these writings, thus giving us a more or less one-sided picture of the medieval doctor.

Developing Professional Ethics

The medical works of the fourteenth century present an especially interesting basis for the study of the development of ethical ideas because they are the first since classical times to contain lengthy and detailed chapters on this subject. These doctors were no longer so inhibited from expressing their own ideas as were the scholastic writers of an earlier century. They were constantly receiving more and better translations of Greek and Arabic medical works, which were the main sources of these ideas, and thus their writings best reveal to us the historical development of the medical code of ethics. . . .

An examination of many of the works of this age and of preceding ones, by placing fourteenth-century writings in their true perspective, shows us why the men of this particular century have a more highly developed professional code; it shows us that their main principles were taken more or less directly from classical writings beginning primarily with the Hippocratic corpus. For even when medicine was yet in its infancy, physicians and surgeons, by their written and spoken words, began to formulate ethical precepts for their fellow-craftsmen, which were repeated by generation after generation of doctors, usually in the introductions to their writings.

A summary of the most important remarks made by these fourteenth-century doctors, as far as possible in their own words, will be used to prove the claims mentioned above. They deal with the qualifications a man must have before he can become a good physician or surgeon, his appearance, his general culture, his relation to and general treatment of his patients, his proper attitude toward other doctors, and, of great importance indeed, his fees.

Appearance

According to [fourteenth century Flemish surgeon] Jan Yperman, the

> doctor must be well-shapen and of a healthy and strong constitution. His outward appearance must be good, for as [ninth-century Persian physician philosopher] al-Rāzī says, an ungainly appearance is not likely to go with a good heart, and [tenth-century Persian physician philosopher] ibn Sīnā says that a fine face will probably hide a fair character. The

surgeon must have shapely hands, taper fingers, and he must be strong. His fingers should not tremble and he must have keen eyesight.

[Late fourteenth-century English surgeon] John of Arderne adds a little to this: "The leech [doctor] should also have clean hands and well-shapen nails cleansed from all blackness and filth." . . .

Deportment and Behavior

It was not enough to be fine-looking and cleanly, but the doctor must also be very careful of his dress and deportment; otherwise he would bring contumely upon himself and his profession. [John of Arderne continues:]

> In clothes and other apparel he should be honest, and not liken himself in apparel and bearing to minstrels, but in clothing and bearing he should show the manner of clerks. For why?; it seemeth any discreet man clad in clerk's garb may occupy the boards of gentlemen. And be he courteous at the lord's table, and be he not displeasing in words or deeds to the guests sitting near by, hear he many things but let him speak but few. . . . And when he shall speak, let the words be short, and as far as possible, fair and reasonable and without swearing. Beware that there never be found double words in his mouth, for if he be found true in his words few or none shall doubt his deeds. . . . Be he not temerarious or boastful in his sayings or in his deeds. And above all this it shall profit him that he always be found sober; for drunkenness destroyeth all virtue and bringeth it to nought. Also let a leech neither laugh nor play too much. . . . Let him be content in strange places with the meats and drinks found there, using measure in all things. . . . Scorn he no man for it is said, "He that scorneth other men shall not go away unscorned.". . . And as far as he can without harm, flee the fellowship of knaves and dishonest persons.

Jan Yperman says about the same things, then adds:

> He ought to devote himself entirely to the patients; in the
> latter's house he may not broach any other subject than that
> which concerns the treatment; neither may he chat with the
> mistress of the house, the daughter or the maidservant, nor
> look at them with leering eyes. For people are soon suspi-
> cious, and by such things he is apt to incur enmity while the
> doctor had better keep on friendly terms with them. . . .

Reputation

The doctors themselves knew that their reputations were not
all they should be, and in all the deontological chapters they
warn against those persons who would make infamous proposals to doctors because [as early fourteenth-century French
surgeon Henri de Mondeville states] from "time immemorial
it has been an article of faith with the common people that
every surgeon is a thief, a murderer or a swindler." No wonder
that so many of their books have stressed the idea that they
must do everything in their power to be of good repute in all
things. That they have succeeded in making their profession
one of the most honored in all countries goes without saying.

Training and Education

Unfortunately these chapters on ethical matters do not go into
detail on the subject of a doctor's education, but they all warn
their readers against illiterate practitioners who wish to treat
the art of medicine as a rude handicraft. Most of a fourteenth-
century doctor's knowledge had to come from books and university lectures, although they could inspect cases in a few
hospitals such as St. Bartholomew's in London and could ac-
company older practitioners on their professional visits. Hence
the translations of Greek and Arabic works as well as the writings of contemporaries and immediate predecessors were of
utmost importance to doctors young and old, although
Mondeville gives the timely warning that "too much faith in

books chokes natural talent." That he must have a fairly broad education is evident from several different sources.

> He must not only have knowledge of medicine, but he must also know the books of nature, which is called philosophy. Grammar, logic, rhetoric and ethics are the four sciences which are necessary to examine things judiciously. With the help of logic things can be tested reasonably; grammar gives us the meaning of the words in Latin, rhetoric teaches us to talk properly, as we hear from the philologers, who however have not acquired this art from books, but by practice. The doctor must also know ethics, as this science teaches good morals. . . .

The Risks of Taking Responsibility for Patients' Health

Cases were not always accepted by reputable physicians in classical and medieval times. According to Mondeville,

> a surgeon ought to be fairly bold. He ought not to quarrel before the laity, and although he should operate wisely and prudently, he should never undertake any dangerous operation unless he is sure that it is the only way to avoid a greater danger. . . . He ought to promise a cure to every sick person, but he should refuse as far as possible all dangerous cases, and he should never accept desperately sick ones.

The reasons for such remarks have often been misinterpreted by our own writers and editors, who claim that it was only because these earlier doctors had a selfish and cowardly desire to escape all blame and criticism. A careful analysis of these fourteenth-century works and a study of their sources show that this fear is not merely a personal one but is professional as well—the laity were already too prone to distrust the medics, and, if the latter promised cures when they knew the case to be a hopeless one, this distrust would be increased. . . .

If a doctor has accepted a case that he later realizes is undoubtedly going to prove fatal, there are two alternatives: he may refuse to continue the treatment or "if the relatives still insist on continuing the treatment, do not neglect to inform them in good time of the impending calamity, for if the end would be fatal you shall not be blamed and shall retain their friendship."

Treating the Whole Patient

Of equal importance with medical care in effecting cures was the state of mind of the patient. Each writer has his own ideas on the methods to be employed to bring about the correct mental condition, but all agree that few diseases can be overcome if the patient is in the wrong frame of mind. First of all one can begin improving the mental state of the patient [Mondeville writes] "by music of viols and ten-stringed psaltery, or by forged letters describing the death of his enemies, or if he is a churchman by telling him that he has been elected to a bishopric."

Always warn the patient that the cure will take a long time, in fact make it twice as long as you really think it will be so that the patient will not be in despair. Then if the patient recovers sooner and

> considers or wonders or asks why he was told the time of curing would be longer, say that it was because the patient was strong hearted, and suffered well sharp things, and that he was of good complexion, and had able flesh to heal; and feign other causes pleasing to the patient, for patients are made proud and delighted by such words. . . .

Connected with the problem of the proper conduct of the physician in regard to their patients is the obedience of the patient and what the doctor should do to obtain it. . . .

[. . . According to Mondeville] There will be no cure if the surgeon does not believe "that the patient has confidence in him and will obey him, otherwise the surgeon cannot visit him with the proper solicitude." Also a doctor should not accept a case [John of Arderne writes] if the patient imagines that neither confidence, obedience, nor the surgical operation will be of any benefit, unless the doctor states in advance the danger to be feared [from this lack of confidence]; or that he is persuaded to accept it by supplications, a large fee, and unless the nurses and friends of the patient consider the doctor shall be entirely and absolutely exonerated from all the accidents which might happen.

Second Opinions and Professional Disagreements

The patient must be warned against consulting more than one doctor at a time because, if he calls in a crowd of them, there will be endless disagreements and different suggestions, and in the meantime the patient will suffer from lack of care. However, the doctor or the patient may call in two or three for a consultation, but it is better if one doctor who seems to know the most about the case should continue the treatment alone.

The doctors are warned against professional jealousy; if a doctor is asked about a colleague, he "should neither set him at nought nor praise him overmuch but should courteously answer: 'I have very little knowledge of him but I have learned nothing but of his goodness and honesty,' and thus shall the honor be increased for each one." . . .

Another obligation put upon the attending doctor is to see that his patient has proper and careful nursing. [Mondeville writes:]

> If the assistants [attendants or relatives] are not careful and conscientious, and are not obedient to the doctor in every possible way they will set at nought the work of the surgeon. . . .

Preventive Medicine

But taking care of the sick was not the only duty of a true physician for he must also advise his people how to prevent ill health. . . . John of Mirfield, an English physician of the first half of the fourteenth century, said that people should not only follow a proper diet to maintain good health but that they should also have plenty of exercise, preferably out of doors. . . .

Medical Fees

In regard to the problem of determining the fees for each case and the manner of collecting them, one must admit that the fourteenth-century attitude on this ever delicate subject, although a little more considerate than that of the two preceding centuries, was not up to the standard set by the Hippocratic ideal. Medieval physicians were seldom shy in admitting in their works that they often charged high fees and became very wealthy from their practice. As John of Arderne says:

> And if he sees that the patient is busily following the cure, then after inquiring about the state of his health, ask boldly for more or less [in fees]; but be he ever wary of scarce asking, for over scarce asking setteth at nought both the market and the thing.

That they were often avaricious is evident from many sources, sometimes even from the frank confessions of the doctors themselves. . . .

These fourteenth-century medical ideals can best be summed up in the words of one of their own doctors [Guy de Chauliac]:

> I say that the doctor should be well mannered, bold in many ways, fearful of dangers, that he should abhor the false cures or practices. He should be affable to the sick, kindhearted to his colleagues, wise in his prognostications. He should be chaste, sober, compassionate and merciful: he should not be covetous, grasping in money matters, and then he will receive a salary commensurate with his labors, the financial ability of his patients, the success of the treatment, and his own dignity.

Enlightenment Moral Philosophy Changes Doctor-Patient Relationships

Laurence B. McCullough

The eighteenth-century Enlightenment was a period of questioning assumptions previously taken for granted and developing new theories to explain new realities. During this time of introspection, moral philosophy was applied to science and medicine. In the following selection, Laurence McCullough reviews the important contribution made to medical ethics by John Gregory during the Scottish Enlightenment. As McCollough writes, medicine in the early 1700s was chaotic and competitive. Patients did not trust physicians and often would consult numerous physicians during an illness. In addition, to avoid taking blame for death, physicians would dismiss any patient who appeared to be beyond help. John Gregory utilized the new moral philosophies developed by David Hume to create new ethical standards in patient care. The central application of Hume's philosophy was the recognition that a physician needed to feel sympathy for his patients. According to McCullough, when physicians began showing concern for patients' well-being instead of focusing solely on curing disease, the doctor-patient relationship changed. Trust between physician and patient increase, and this allowed honest and open communication between them. For example, through an understanding of the patient's end of life needs, physicians could provide honest assessments of medical status and continue to treat dying patients without being blamed for their death.

Laurence McCullough is a professor of medicine and medical ethics at Baylor University and a faculty associate of Baylor's

Laurence B. McCullough, "Bioethics in the Twenty-first Century: Why We Should Pay Attention to Eighteenth-century Medical Ethics," *Kennedy Institute of Ethics Journal*, vol. 6, 1996, pp. 329–333. Copyright © 1996 by the Johns Hopkins University Press. Reproduced by permission.

Huffington Center on Aging, where he leads the Ethics Research Group. He has published more than 150 articles and original book chapters, as well as numerous textbook chapters including John Gregory and the Invention of Professional Medical Ethics and the Profession of Medicine.

Those of us who work in the field of bioethics tend to think that, because the word "bioethics" is new, so too the field is new in all respects, but we are not the first to do bioethics. John Gregory (1724–1773) did bioethics just as we do it, at least two centuries before we thought to do it. He deployed philosophical methods as sophisticated as our own. Indeed, Gregory took up the very best moral philosophy available to thinkers of the Scottish Enlightenment, namely, David Hume's moral philosophy and its core concept of sympathy. Gregory also responded in a conceptually powerful and clinically applicable way to the problems of his time, just as we do. I want here to outline Gregory's accomplishment and to identify some aspects of its importance for bioethics in the twenty-first century.

A Competitive, Chaotic Discipline

Gregory wrote his medical ethics as a response to the then current state of medicine in Britain. We now follow Gregory in our writing of bioethics and clinical ethics in response to the problems of our time. A great deal that we now take for granted did not then exist.

There was not, as there is now, any uniform pathway into medicine. Nor did there exist universal licensure. The Royal Colleges did attempt to assert, but failed to achieve, monopoly control of medical practice. The concepts of health and disease were themselves contested and therefore competed for their success in the market place. There was a marked over-supply of practitioners who competed fiercely—very fiercely indeed—in the medical market place for their concepts of health and disease, their treatments, and therefore their livelihoods. Patients had their own concepts of health and disease, engaged in "self-physicking" or self-care, and often traded physician's prescriptions.

Medicine exhibited little scientific discipline in its accounts of disease and in determining the efficacy of treatments, a fact that Gregory laments as a medical student. There was no marked improvement when he began to give his medical ethics lectures nearly a quarter of a century later. Treatments failed as often, perhaps more often, than they succeeded in benefiting patients. The sick usually sought out the help of a physician after trying self-physicking.

Physicians, Gregory taught, could not hope to *control* human biology, though they could aim to manage its processes well. When nature underresponds to disease the physician should assist her processes; when nature overresponds, the physician should tamp down nature's responses, to lessen their "violence"—in both cases always attentive to the limits of medicine's capacities in treating disease.

Physicians attended the well-to-do sick at home, and the sick person summoned and dismissed physicians, surgeons, or apothecaries at will. A physician therefore might find himself—no women had yet been admitted to the ranks of university-trained physicians—summoned before, after, or simultaneously with a competitor, with his concepts and diagnosis and treatment put to the acid test. In this setting, there existed only a patient-physician relationship, not a physician-patient relationship.

Physicians left off the care of dying patients, a practice that was made a matter of duty by Friederich Hoffmann [a late seventeenth-century physician]. One would suffer punishing economic consequences if one had a high mortality rate. Better, then, to label the patient incurable, withdraw, and turn matters over to clergy. Gregory attacks this practice as intellectual fraud and calls for the physician to continue to attend the dying. Indeed, he says, "It is as much the business of a physician to alleviate pain, and to smooth the avenues of death, when unavoidable, as to cure diseases". He does not explicitly address what we now call physician-assisted suicide; neither does he condemn it, and he is quick to condemn some things—e.g., sexual abuse of female patients or "sporting" with patients in the Royal Infirmary by using experiments as the first line of treatment.

Substandard Medical Care for the Poor

The Royal Infirmary was established to care for the deserving, working poor, who received free care. The sick had first to obtain a ticket of admission from one of the benefactors of the Infirmary and then pass screening by the lay managers of the institution, who selected against patients with "fever" or any other sign of life-threatening illness, to keep mortality rates down. Thus, a not-for-profit institution invented market segmentation for the purpose of advancing institutional self-interest. The lay managers exerted strict control of resources and complained regularly of the overuse of resources and high mortality rates on the teaching ward.

There were regular accusations of callousness made against the physicians of the Infirmary, who were appointed by the benefactors and served without recompense. Physicians, Gregory says, abused the label "incurable" by applying it too quickly, so as to rationalize the use of experiments as the first line of treatment. Institutional support existed for an emerging physician-patient relationship, but as yet there was no ethics to guide and regulate the growing power of physicians in this new institution.

All of these problems combined to create a crisis of confidence, on the part of the sick, in those who put themselves forward as medical practitioners. "Whom can I trust?" became an urgent question for the sick in a medical market place driven largely, often exclusively, by the physician's pursuit of self-interest. Medicine, Gregory feared, had become commercial, a trade or means to the end of the physicians's self-interest. Gregory, deeply under the influence of the fading, Highland ideals, railed against commerce in general and commerce in medicine in particular.

Incorporating Sympathy into Medical Ethics

Gregory utilizes the great invention of Scottish Enlightenment philosophy, Hume's moral sense philosophy of sympathy, to address these and other problems. His topic list includes: truth-telling to the seriously ill; confidentiality, especially with regard to female patients; sexual abuse of female patients; consultations, including negotiating the then very unstable borders between medicine and surgery and between physicians and apothecaries, mistakenly thought by some commentators to involve mere etiquette; abandoning dying patients; the abuse of patients for experimentation; animal experimentation; and the definition and clinical determination of death. This topic list anticipates much of what we now take to be "new" problems. In what follows, I consider his method for moral philosophy and its consequence, the invention of the ethical concept of the physician as the moral fiduciary of the patient.

Gregory was steeped in Scottish moral sense philosophy, having studied and accepted Hume's moral philosophy while he was teaching at King's College in the 1750's, during which time he helped to found and played a very active role in the proceedings of the Aberdeen Philosophical Society. Numerous sessions of the Society were devoted to the critical study and discussion of Hume's *A Treatise of Human Nature*. Gregory absorbed and accepted the central concept in Hume's moral philosophy, sympathy, which had a technical meaning for Hume that was well understood and accepted in his time.

The virtues of properly functioning sympathy are tenderness and steadiness. Women of learning and virtue, Gregory believed, provide the moral exemplars of these virtues—particularly women of the London Bluestocking Circle [an eighteenth-century organization that stressed women's intellectual and social prowess], especially Mrs. Elizabeth Montagu. To use current terminology, Gregory genders sympathy as feminine, thus writing the first feminine medical ethics long before theories of care based on affiliative or relational psychology.

Gregory thus writes the first philosophical, secular, professional, clinical, and feminine medical ethics in the English-language literature of medical ethics. He did so just as we do, by bringing to bear the methodological tools of philosophy on the actual problems encountered by physicians and health care institutions. In doing so, he solves a very serious problem for the medicine of this day, its lack of professional character in the ethical sense. Gregory took the view that medicine involved a life of service and sacrifice in the care of patients— the physician as moral fiduciary.

A Nineteenth-Century Physician Develops a Modern Formal Code of Medical Ethics

Thomas Percival

Thomas Percival was an English physician, scholar, and philosopher of the late eighteenth and early nineteenth centuries England. Percival laid the groundwork for modern biomedical ethics with his comprehensive evaluation of the eighteenth-century British medical system. The following selection contains a portion of Thomas Percival's innovative work, Medical Ethics. *In this excerpt, Percival discusses the behavior, training, medical fees, and medical practices he feels are required in order to be a competent and ethical physician or surgeon. The ground-breaking* Medical Ethics *was used as the basis for the American Medical Association's Code of Ethics. In addition to his master-work,* Medical Ethics, *Percival published articles on medicine and science in the journal* Philosophical Transactions *and wrote pamphlets about hospital regulations and professional conduct.*

The *moral rules of conduct*, prescribed towards hospital patients, should be fully adopted in private or general practice. Every case, committed to the charge of a physician or surgeon, should be treated with attention, steadiness, and humanity: Reasonable indulgence should be granted to the mental imbecility and caprices of the sick: Secrecy, and delicacy when required by peculiar circumstances, should be strictly observed. And the familiar and confidential intercourse, to which the faculty [i.e., trained professional physicians] are ad-

Thomas Percival, *Medical Ethics or A Code of Institutes and Precepts Adapted to the Professional Conduct of Physicians and Surgeons.* Manchester, UK: S. Russell, 1803, pp. 30–52.

mitted in their professional visits, should be used with discretion, and with the most scrupulous regard to fidelity and honour.

Temperance and Truthfulness

The strictest *temperance* should be deemed incumbent on the faculty; as the practice both of physic and surgery at all times requires the exercise of a clear and vigorous understanding: And on emergencies, for which no professional man should be unprepared, a steady hand, an acute eye, and an unclouded head, may be essential to the well being, and even to the life, of a fellow-creature. . . .

A physician should not be forward to make gloomy prognostications; because they savour of empiricism, by magnifying the importance of his services in the treatment or cure of the disease. But he should not fail, on proper occasions, to give to the friends of the patient, timely notice of danger, when it really occurs, and even to the patient himself, if absolutely necessary. . . .

Proper Behavior Towards Colleagues

Officious interference, in a case under the charge of another, should be carefully avoided. . . .

When a physician or surgeon is called to a patient, who has been before under the care of another gentleman of the faculty, a consultation with him should be even proposed, though he may have discontinued his visits: His practice, also, should be treated with candour, and justified, so far as probity and truth will permit. . . .

Education and Training

A regular *academical education* furnishes the only presumptive evidence of professional ability, and is so honourable and beneficial, that it gives a just claim to pre-eminence among physicians, in proportion to the degree in which it has been enjoyed and improved: Yet as it is not indispensably necessary to the attainment of knowledge, skill, and experience, they who have really acquired, in a competent measure, such qualifications, without its advantages, should not be fastidiously excluded from the privileges of fellowship. . . .

Providing the Right Amount of Care

Visits to the sick should not be *unseasonably repeated*; because, when too frequent, they tend to diminish the authority of the physician, to produce instability in his practice, and to give rise to such occasional indulgences, as are subversive of all medical regimen. . . .

Charity

Some general rule should be adopted, by the faculty, in every town, relative to the *pecuniary acknowledgments* [ability to pay] of their patients; and it should be deemed a point of honour to adhere to this rule, with as much steadiness, as varying circumstances will admit. For it is obvious that an average fee, as suited to the general rank of patients, must be an inadequate gratuity from the rich, who often require attendance not absolutely necessary; and yet too large to be expected from that class of citizens, who would feel a reluctance in calling for assistance, without making some decent and satisfactory retribution. . . .

All members of the profession, including apothecaries as well as physicians and surgeons, together with their wives and children, should be attended *gratuitously* by any one or more of the faculty, residing near them, whose assistance may be required. . . .

When a physician attends the wife or child of a member of the faculty, or any person very nearly connected with him, he should manifest peculiar attention to his opinions, and tenderness even to his prejudices. . . .

Cautions Against Deceitful Practices

Physicians and surgeons are occasionally requested to furnish certificates, justifying the absence of persons who hold situations of honour and trust in the army, the navy, or the civil departments of government. These testimonials, unless under particular circumstances, should be considered as acts due to the public, and therefore not to be compenstaed by any gratuity. But they should never be given without an accurate and faithful scrutiny into the case; that truth and probity may not be violated, nor the good of the community injured, by the unjust pretences of its servants. The same conduct is to be observed by medical practitioners, when they are solicited to furnish apologies for non-attendance on juries; or to state the valetudinary incapacity of persons appointed to execute the business of constables, church-wardens, or overseers of the poor. . . .

The use of *quack medicines* should be discouraged by the faculty, as disgraceful to the profession, injurious to health, and often destructive even of life. . . .

No physician or surgeon should dispense a secret *nostrum* [cure], whether it be his invention, or exclusive property. For if it be of real efficacy, the concealment of it is inconsistent with beneficence and professional liberality. And if mystery alone give it value and importance, such craft implies either disgraceful ignorance, or fraudulent avarice.

Professional Unity

The *Esprit du Corps* is a principle of action founded in human nature, and when duly regulated, is both rational and laudable. Every man who enters into a fraternity engages, by a tacit compact, not only to submit to the laws, but to promote the honour and interest of the association, so far as they are consistent with morality, and the general good of mankind. A physician, therefore, should cautiously guard against whatever may injure the general respectability of his profession; and should avoid all contumelious [slanderous] representations of the faculty at large; all general charges against their selfishness or improbity; and the indulgence of an affected or jocular scepticism, concerning the efficacy and utility of the healing art.

As diversity of opinion and opposition of interest may in the medical, as in other professions, sometimes occasion *controversy*, and even *contention*; whenever such cases unfortunately occur, and cannot be immediately terminated, they should be referred to the arbitration of a sufficient number of physicians or of surgeons, according to the nature of the dispute; or to the two orders collectively, if belonging both to medicine and surgery. . . .

Learning From Experience

At the close of every interesting and important case, especially when it hath terminated fatally, a physician should trace back, in calm reflection, all the steps which he had taken in the treatment of it. This review of the origin, progress, and conclusion of the malady; of the whole curative plan pursued; and of the particular operation of the several remedies employed, as well as of the doses and periods of time in which they were administered, will furnish the most authentic documents, on which individual experience can be formed. But it is in a moral view that the practice is here recommended; and it should be performed with the most scrupulous impartiality. Let no self-deception be permitted in the retrospect; and if errors, either of omission or commission, are discovered, it behoves that they should be brought fairly and fully to the mental view. Regrets may follow, but criminality will thus be obviated. For good intentions, and the imperfection of human skill which cannot anticipate the knowledge that events alone disclose, will sufficiently justify what is past, provided the failure be made conscientiously subservient to future wisdom and rectitude in professional conduct. . . .

Retirement

A physician who is advancing in years, yet unconscious of any decay in his faculties, may occasionally experience some change in the wonted confidence of his friends. Patients, who before trusted solely to his care and skill, may now request that he will join in consultation, perhaps with a younger co-adjutor. It behoves him to admit this change without dissatisfaction or fastidiousness, regarding it as no mark of disrespect; but as the exercise of a just and reasonable privilege in those by whom he is employed. The junior practitioner may well be supposed to have more ardour, than he possesses, in the treatment of diseases; to be bolder in the exhibition of new medicines; and disposed to administer old ones in doses of greater efficacy. And this union of enterprize with caution, and of fervour with coolness, may promote the successful management of a difficult and protracted case. . . .

The commencement of that period of senescence [decay], when it becomes incumbent on a physician to decline the offices of his profession, it is not easy to ascertain; and the decision on so nice a point must be left to the moral discretion of the individual. . . . As age advances, therefore, a physician should, from time to time, scrutinize impartially the state of his faculties; that he may determine, *bona fide*, the precise degree in which he is qualified to execute the active and multifarious offices of his profession. And whenever he becomes conscious that his memory presents to him, with faintness, those analogies, on which medical reasoning and the treatment of diseases are founded; that diffidence of the measures to be pursued perplexes his judgment; that, from a deficiency in the acuteness of his senses, he finds himself less able to distinguish signs, or to prognosticate events; he should at once resolve, though others perceive not the changes which have taken place, to sacrifice every consideration of fame or fortune, and to retire from the engagements of business.

CHAPTER 2

Euthanasia and Physician-Assisted Suicide

Chapter Preface

Euthanasia is defined as the deliberate act of helping someone to die in order to relieve suffering, usually from a terminal illness. Euthanasia is broken into two main categories—active and passive—depending upon the role of a physician or an assistant in effecting a patient's death. In passive euthanasia, life-sustaining medical treatment is stopped with the deliberate intention of allowing the patient to die. In active euthanasia, steps must be taken to cause death, such as ingesting an overdose of medication. Another term used frequently in the euthanasia debate is "assisted suicide," which occurs when a doctor provides, but does not administer, the means for a patient to end his or her own life.

The right to perform euthanasia or physician-assisted suicide (PAS) is one of the most hotly debated topics in medical ethics, as it pits individual rights against strongly held beliefs advocating the sanctity of life. For example, in 1991, forty-year-old Sue Rodriguez, a Canadian, was diagnosed with amyotrophic lateral sclerosis (ALS). ALS is a progressive disease that gradually results in the loss of the ability to walk, move body parts at will, eat, and finally breathe without mechanical assistance. During all the stages of ALS, the mind remains alert. After learning about her condition, Rodriguez decided to avoid the final stages of the disease by requesting to die at a time and in a manner of her own choosing under the supervision of a physician. However, PAS was illegal in her home province of British Columbia. Citing her right to choose her manner of death, Rodriguez fought for legalization of PAS in the courts.

Rodriguez's battle did not change Canadian law, and she ultimately chose suicide (with the help of an anonymous physician) to end her life on her own terms in 1994. The legal contest and the media attention, however, forced the public to address the law banning PAS and spurred debate on the euthanasia issue. The following chapter examines the history of euthanasia as well as current debates over assisted-suicide legislation and ethics.

Christian Doctrine Condemns the Ancient Practice of Euthanasia

Ian Robert Dowbiggin

The term euthanasia derives from the Greek for "good death." In ancient Greek and Roman times, euthanasia was the equivalent of today's physician-assisted suicide and was considered an ethically appropriate and rational option for those facing pain, dishonor, or execution. Physicians routinely supplied patients with poisons to help them commit suicide or quicken their deaths. In the following selection, Ian Robert Dowbiggin traces the transformation in the public's ethical view of this form of euthanasia from the ancient pagan times to the middle ages. As the Christian doctrine upholding the sanctity of life spread over Roman territory, Dowbiggin writes, the concept of euthanasia as ethical was countered by the notion that life was "God's gift" in which men should not interfere. Christian theologians held that euthanasia and physician-assisted suicide were against God's plan and therefore a serious sin and a major crime. Dowbiggin notes that christians were also taught that suffering from a prolonged painful illness allowed the individual to emulate the suffering of Christ and would provide sanctification. The taboo on physician-assisted suicide persisted until the eighteenth century when the Enlightenment opened up hidebound Christian doctrine to debate.

Ian Robert Dowbiggin is a history professor and the department chair of history at the University of Prince Edward Island. He is the author of four books including A Merciful End: The Euthanasia Movement in Modern America.

Ian Robert Dowbiggin, *A Concise History of Euthanasia: Life, Death, God, and Medicine.* Lanham MD: Rowman & Littlefield Publishers, Inc., 2005, pp. 7–26. Copyright © 2005 by Rowman & Littlefield Publishers, Inc. All rights reserved. Reproduced by permission.

The story is told by Pliny the Younger (62–114 A.D.), the renowned Roman writer, lawyer, orator, and administrator. Sketchy in detail, the tale nonetheless says a great deal about the nonjudgmental attitude of the ancient Romans toward the question of what constituted a "good death." . . .

As Pliny the Younger told the story, a certain man was suffering from an unspecified disease of the genital organs. His wife asked to see the affected part. Having satisfied her curiosity, she promptly declared his condition to be incurable and deadly. Her advice was that the couple should jointly commit suicide by drowning, though there is no indication that the husband ardently shared her opinion. Whatever his intentions, they ended up throwing themselves into a lake together.

This story of a suicide pact between a husband and wife is only one of many tales of suicide in classical antiquity. Many ancient Greek and Roman philosophers considered suicide a "good death," an appropriate and rational response to a wide variety of circumstances. There are numerous accounts of people killing themselves by poison, fasting, asphyxiation, hanging, or slitting their wrists. Motives ran the gamut from pains due to cancer, bladder stones, stomach disorders, gout, and headaches, to melancholy, the fear of dishonor, and the hope of avoiding judgment and execution. Individuals frequently asked their physicians to either supply them with the means of suicide (assisted suicide) or actually hasten their deaths through medical intervention (active voluntary euthanasia), for example by administering poison. Quite simply, assisting suicide and mercy killing were common and tolerated practices in ancient Greece and early imperial Rome.

Suicide and euthanasia were common acts in classical antiquity because fundamentally they did not conflict with the moral beliefs of the time. The ancients were fairly permissive about self-murder and euthanasia. In stark contrast to the teaching of most modern-day Christian churches, Jewish religious bodies, and other world religions, the ancient Greeks and Romans did not think that all human life had an inherent value. They tended to reject any semblance of the belief in the sanctity of human life, or the modern notion that all people enjoyed a range of natural rights by virtue of a universal property of their human condition. When faced with hopeless circumstances, the ancient Greeks and Romans suffered little social disapproval if they chose to end their lives, commit infanticide, or perform abortions. . . .

The Hippocratic Oath

Perhaps the most important aspect of the story told by Pliny the Younger is that he offered no moral opinion about the act of suicide. His suspension of judgment indicates that such events were fairly routine and often drew little comment. If Pliny's opinions about suicide were in any way indicative of reality, they help to explain why the Hippocratic Oath forbade the participation of physicians in acts designed to shorten the lives of patients. Little is known precisely about the oath's origins, but it is generally thought to be the product of more than one solitary physician called Hippocrates and to date from between the fifth and third centuries BC. Before the Christian era, it did not draw much attention from physicians or other people. Its value as a historical document is that it sheds light on what likely passed for customary medical practice.

Among its several injunctions is the first clear denunciation of mercy killing or assisted suicide in Western medical history. The Hippocratic body of writings contains several references encouraging physicians to refrain from life-prolonging treatment if the patient is dying. The oath also reads: "I will not give a fatal drug to anyone if I am asked, nor will I suggest any such thing." The oath's authority has resonated down through the ages to the present day, when physicians swear to the god Apollo to keep the oath to the best of their "ability and judgment." The Hippocratic Oath is a milestone in the history of medicine because it articulated the lofty goals of the selfless doctor who would inspire later generations of physicians, a model of professional competence and probity. It also strongly expressed the theory that physicians should look for the causes of and remedies for disease in purely natural explanations of sickness. But the oath's blanket prohibition against euthanasia (and abortion) has met increasing resistance in recent years.

Two things can be said about the oath with some assurance: first, many ancient Greek and Roman physicians did not abide by its injunctions, and second, the oath's prohibition of euthanasia plainly was a kind of protest against the frequency with which euthanasia was practiced in the years before the revolutionary coming of Christianity. There never would have been a need for the oath's injunction if euthanasia had been rare in the first place. The oath's influence became powerful only in later centuries. In the meantime, it confirmed the prevailing belief in classical antiquity that there was nothing inconsistent between the values of that day and physician-assisted suicide or actual medical mercy killing.

Judaism and Euthanasia

The attitude of ancient Romans and Greeks in favor of medical assistance in dying steadily met resistance in the first centuries of the common era, thanks to two formidable forces in world history. The first was Judaism. In the words of the Central Conference of American Rabbis in 1972, "the Jewish ideal of the sanctity of human life and the supreme value of the individual soul would suffer incalculable harm if, contrary to the moral law, men were at liberty to determine the conditions under which they might put an end to their own lives and the lives of other men." As late as 1997, even Reform Judaism, the most liberal of all branches of Judaism, refused to declare that euthanasia was consistent with Jewish values.

The reasons for the firm Jewish religious opposition to both assisted suicide and mercy killing are sprinkled throughout the Jewish scriptures. which constitute the Christian Old Testament. On multiple occasions in the Old Testament, God is acknowledged to exercise an absolute sovereignty over life and death. Death was the penalty for sin, and life was a gift from God that his people were meant to choose so they could continue to love, honor, and obey him. Choosing death was an affront to God that demonstrated contempt for the gift of life: "No man has authority . . . over the day of death" (Ecclesiastes 8:8). The scriptures contain some examples of Jews willingly dying as martyrs or choosing suicide, but they do so because they prefer death to violating Judaic law. And none of these examples occurs in conditions remotely resembling the circumstances surrounding modern-day medical euthanasia or physician-assisted suicide. Throughout the Old Testament, there is no instance of Jews either killing themselves or arranging for someone else to help them die due to the physical anguish of illness.

These firm Jewish beliefs about suicide and euthanasia spread throughout the Roman imperial world thanks to the huge Jewish diaspora. Even before the catastrophe of 66–70 A.D., when a large-scale Jewish revolt was crushed mercilessly by the Romans and the Temple in Jerusalem was destroyed by the imperial armies, the Jews were a powerful presence throughout the Mediterranean region. Sizeable communities could be found in cities such as Alexandria, Antioch, Damascus, and even Rome itself. Jewish value systems probably had little effect on pagan Romans. But when they became synthesized with the beliefs of the growing numbers of Christian converts sprinkled throughout the Roman Empire, they steadily shaped public attitudes as the new millennium wore on.

The Coming of Christianity

The emergence of Christianity in the first century A.D. was the other momentous factor that shaped the new era in the history of euthanasia. Basic Christian values about death and dying are similar to the Judaic moral code, although explicit condemnations of suicide are missing from the New Testament. It was in later centuries that the church fathers inferred from the Gospels that suicide was against God's law. A major spokesperson for this theory was Saint Augustine (354–430 A.D.), who in his *City of God* (428) argued that suicide was simply another form of homicide, and thus was both a crime and a sin prohibited by the sixth of the Ten Commandments. In Augustine's eyes, even those who opted for suicide in order to avoid a sin (such as a virgin seeking to protect her virtue) were actually committing greater sin and forfeited the possibility of repentance. . . .

In the early centuries of the new millennium, the attitude of Christians toward life and death was that human beings inhabited a fallen world in which suffering had to be endured as the penalty of sin. The life we enjoy is a gift from God, who remains sovereign over all things, and any effort to end existence through suicide or aid in dying is a shameful attempt to escape the trials that God in his wisdom has decided to inflict or permit. Allowances sometimes were made for suicides during a state of mental illness. But, in the end analysis, Christians were taught to be "obedient unto death," in Saint Paul's words (see Philippians 2:5–11). Suffering emulated the suffering of Christ and provided human beings with an opportunity to sanctify their lives. . . .

Euthanasia in the Middle Ages

After the collapse of the Roman Empire, and as the Middle Ages unfolded over the next one thousand years, any semblance of ancient approval for suicide or mercy killing vanished throughout the Western world. The Christian view that suicide was a serious sin and major crime took root steadily, and it ultimately became so accepted in the medieval mind that there existed virtually no debate over the subject. The anti-suicide consensus was reflected in clerical doctrine and secular literature and law. Any doubts about the acceptability of suicide were erased during the medieval era by the spectacle of the severe punishments meted out to the bodies of suicides and their surviving families. . . .

The medieval age also witnessed a distinct change in the practice of medicine, a shift that further undercut the ancient permissiveness toward suicide and euthanasia. . . .

In the midst of the elaborate and deeply emotional drama surrounding death, the physician was forbidden to do anything that might detract from the spiritual journey the patient was undertaking. Any medical hastening of the dying process was strictly prohibited. However, there is no evidence physicians objected. Because they were so limited in their therapeutic power anyway, they tended to embrace, their role as bedside participant in the ceremony surrounding a Christian "good death." Whatever their individual religious convictions, they knew that concern for the patient's personal life and general well-being signaled an important part of their fundamental contribution to the death-bed ritual. . . .

As the Middle Ages began to fade and the effects of the Renaissance started to be felt, a clear collective attitude toward suicide and euthanasia emerged. The medieval consensus was not without nuances. But the medieval mind, by conflating suicide, euthanasia, and the sixth commandment ("thou shalt not kill"), found it difficult to condone hastening a death, either by someone else's or one's own hands. By the onset of the sixteenth century, church, state, society, and medicine had forged an alliance that decisively rejected the taking of a life either by suicide or with medical assistance. This durable alliance would weather the Renaissance, the Reformation, and even the Enlightenment, lasting for the most part down to the early twentieth century. Only then would the venerable Christian consensus regarding a good death begin to unravel. . . .

Euthanasia Becomes a Political Issue in the United States

Peter G. Filene

In the late 1800s and early 1900s, the euthanasia debate in the United States moved from the medical profession into the courts and political forums. The attempts to legalize euthanasia began as physicians increased their ability to prolong the life of terminally ill patients in the early twentieth century. Several bills were passed to try and legalize euthanasia. However, as Peter G. Filene notes in the following selection, they all failed as critics began to frame euthanasia not as a patient's wish but as a doctor's questionable decision to commit murder. Further debate was stalled, Filene states, until a shift in terminology after World War II equated euthanasia with the "mercy killing" of feeble-minded or otherwise impaired persons. With this negative connotation, euthanasia fell out of favor, and new debates surfaced over physicians' duties, patients' rights, and the rights of relatives to act on the behalf of loved ones who were comatose. Peter G. Filene is a professor of history at the University of North Carolina. He has published several books and articles including In the Arms of Others: A Cultural History of the Right-to-Die in America.

Before the twentieth century they talked in terms of *euthanasia*, but they didn't have in mind what we think of today. Euthanasia has come to mean hastening the death of hopelessly suffering patients—"mercy killing"—or, in a more sinister connotation, killing people deemed unfit or defective. To nineteenth-century Americans, on the other hand, euthanasia referred less to the physician's action than to the experience of his patient. "A good death"—that is the literal translation from the Greek term coined by Francis Bacon in the seventeenth century. The question was how best to provide such a death, painless and easy, to someone who was terminally ill.

The newly formed American Medical Association, in its 1847 code of ethics, called upon doctors to comfort but, whenever possible, also to revive. "The physician should be the minister of hope and comfort to the sick, that by such cordials to the drooping spirit, he may soothe the bed of death, revive expiring life, and counteract the depressing influence of those maladies which often disturb the tranquillity of the most resigned in their last moments...."

In practice, however, most nineteenth-century doctors believed that they would best minister and soothe a dying patient by letting nature take its course. "... We dismiss all thought of cure, or of the prolongation of life," British Dr. William Munk declared in his influential textbook *Euthanasia* (1887), "and our efforts are limited to the relief of certain urgent conditions, such as pain...." "Where there is no hope ...," a Philadelphia surgeon agreed in 1894, "it should be a grateful and sacred duty, nay, it should be the highest triumph of the physician to minister unto the wants of a dying fellow creature by effecting the Euthanasia." In an era when most people died at home rather than in a hospital, physicians were expected to join the family circle around the death-bed and comfort with sympathetic words and gentle touch....

If the pain grew unbearable, doctors typically administered opium, morphine, alcohol, or some other analgesic, as large a dose as needed for a peaceful passing. Contrary to later medical fears of addicting their patients, Victorian physicians believed that "the risk of the drug habit sinks into insignificance in the presence of approaching death." As a renowned American surgeon said during a public symposium in 1913, "Others have assumed the responsibility which I myself have taken in more than one case, of producing euthanasia."

The Medical Ability to Prolong Life Stimulates Euthanasia Debate

By the early twentieth century, through, most people no longer argued about producing euthanasia but about committing it. The focus had shifted from the patient's state of mind to the doctor's decision whether or not to hasten death. The paradox of medical progress was beginning to emerge. The more successful physicians became in curing disease and prolonging life, the more they were also held accountable for prolonging suffering. As the president of the American Bar Association, Judge Simeon E. Baldwin, declared in a widely publicized address at the turn of the century: "In civilized nations, and particularly of late years, it has become the pride of many in the medical profession to prolong such life [of terminally ill patients] at any cost of discomfort or pain to the sufferer or of expense and exhaustion to his family." Baldwin called instead for "the natural right to a natural death."

A few years later an Ohio state legislator went a step further, introducing a bill to legalize euthanasia. If a person of sound mind was suffering extreme pain from a fatal injury or terminal illness, and if a physician asked whether he wanted to die and the patient said yes, then (after three other physicians agreed that recovery was hopeless) the physician could administer a fatal dose of anesthetic. Not surprisingly, the bill never got out of committee. More important, though it defined euthanasia not as a patient's easy death or natural death but as his doctor's action to bring about death. The physician who could not save life was supposed to end it. With the issue framed this way, the public responded in like terms. "Shall we legalize homicide?" the editors of *Outlook* asked in terms that left no doubt as to their answer. *The Independent* berated "the awful frank cruelty and crudity" of this plan for "legalizing the taking of human life. . . ." Leading newspapers in New York, Boston, and Philadelphia, joined by spokespersons of the Catholic church, added their indignant objections. The good death had been turned into murder.

The Euthanasia Society of America Works to Legalize Euthanasia

Later efforts to legalize euthanasia imprinted even more deeply this negative connotation. In 1938 various social reformers, physicians, and academics founded the Euthanasia Society of America (ESA). . . . The next year they sponsored a bill in the New York state legislature along the lines of the one in Ohio. No legislator was willing to sponsor it, and what little public response it evoked was hostile. Still, the ESA took heart from an opinion poll reporting that 46 percent of Americans favored "mercy deaths under Government supervision for hopeless invalids." But soon the concept of euthanasia took on more sinister implications. By 1941 news was filtering out of Germany that the Nazi regime had established a program whereby medical personnel put to death mentally retarded children, crippled and ill people, the elderly, and others with "lives not worth living." In other words, euthanasia was being joined with eugenics, the policy of race breeding by weeding out "the unfit."

The ESA frantically tried to explain to the public that its purposes—voluntary euthanasia—had nothing in common with the Nazis' program of involuntary euthanasia. The fact was, however, that most ESA leaders were longtime ardent believers in eugenics. Until now they had kept that side of their ideology discreetly in the background. But their president was candid enough in public statements. "Now my face is set against the legalization of euthanasia for any person, who, having been well, has at last become ill, for however ill they be, many get well and help the world for years after," Dr. Foster Kennedy explained. "But I *am* in favor of euthanasia for those hopeless ones who should never have been born— Nature's mistakes." The feebleminded, idiots and imbeciles, "the completely hopeless defective," said Kennedy, "should be relieved of the burden of living. . . ." Such ideas were already considered cranky and outmoded. When the world learned the horrific facts of the Holocaust, they became unspeakable. The Euthanasia Society nevertheless stubbornly continued trying to organize state chapters, sponsor legislation, and publicize its beliefs, but by 1960 it had virtually ground to a halt. Eugenics, one historian has written, had become "virtually a dirty word," and euthanasia was irremediably sullied along with it.

A Change in Language Shifts Attitudes Towards Euthanasia

Advocates of physicians ending the hopeless suffering of terminally ill patients needed to clothe their ideas in a different vocabulary: the language of mercy. If euthanasia were performed as a merciful action, it might be justifiable. Between 1930 and 1960, cases of "mercy killings" made news again and again, arousing widespread fascination and moral debate. John Stephens in Atlanta bashed his sixty-year-old aunt in the head with a flower pot to end her agony from terminal cancer. A coroner's jury exonerated him, saying she had died of natural causes. . . .

But these were the actions of desperate individuals—vigilante euthanasia, one might say. The action of Dr. Hermann Sander, by contrast, evoked Americans' attitudes toward official euthanasia—end-of-life treatment by the medical profession. In December 1949 the 40-year-old New Hampshire doctor was charged with murder after injecting ten cc. of air into the vein of his unconscious patient, Abbie Borroto, and then repeating the process three times until, ten minutes later, she was dead. Mrs. Borroto, 59 years old, had been bedridden for months with terminal cancer, dwindling from 140 to 80 pounds and, Sander later said, clearly within hours of death. Dr. Sander "is a fine man," said the county solicitor, "a good family man, without a malicious bone in his body: he just thought he was performing an act of mercy." Six hundred of the 650 residents in Sander's hometown signed a petition expressing confidence in him. The Congregational minister in nearby Manchester declared: "If this man is felonious then so am I, for I have desired the time of suffering to be short and I have wanted natural and unaided courses to bring relief in death." The Reverend Billy Graham, on the other hand, told an audience of 6,000 people in Boston that Sander should be punished "as an example," a sentiment echoed by various Protestant ministers and even more strongly by Catholic spokesmen.

By the time the Sander trial began, according to *Time* magazine, "the nation's interest in 'mercy killing' [had been] quickened," producing discussions in corner drugstores and church pulpits. Letters to local New Hampshire newspapers were so inflammatory, pro and con, that the editors decided to stop printing them. One hundred and fifty reporters and photographers arrived in Manchester, some from as far as London, including novelists John O'Hara and Fanny Hurst. The trial lasted fourteen days, during which time the press sent out almost as many words per day as during the trial of Bruno Hauptmann, kidnaper of the Lindberghs' baby.

After the prosecutor introduced detailed evidence of murder (including Sander's dictated case notes of the injections), expert witnesses for the defense argued that forty cc. of air was insufficient to cause death and that Mrs. Borroto died from cancer and pneumonia. Sander himself denied he had sought to kill her. "As I looked at her face and all of the thoughts of the past went through my mind, something snapped in me, and I felt impelled or possessed to do something, I couldn't have been thinking the way I ordinarily do or I wouldn't have acted this way."

In the end, the all-male jury deliberated only seventy minutes before deciding that Dr. Sander was not guilty of malice afore-thought and deliberation, and that Mrs. Borroto's death had not been caused by the injections. "It was the most heart-warming news I have ever received," said her husband, Reginald Borroto. That night a crowd of five hundred supporters marched in torch-light parade past the Sanders' white farmhouse.

The furor surrounding the trial signaled how strongly Americans cared about treatment of the dying. Even more telling were the words people used. "Euthanasia is *not* the defense," Sander's lawyer insisted. The *New York Times Index* classified its articles under "Mercy Death (Euthanasia)." Most often, whether they opposed or supported what the doctor had done, people called it "mercy killing." The liberal *New Republic* had another suggestion. "If we called these situations 'assisted suicide' rather than 'mercy killing,' the moral context would be considerably changed."

Terminology was in flux because attitudes were in transition. Although the law and the code of medical ethics forbade a doctor from committing euthanasia, even as an act of mercy, more and more Americans—including some doctors—began insisting that patients deserved to be freed from hopeless suffering. "There has been too little said of a legitimate right, a God-given right, of the dying man," a San Francisco general practitioner stated in 1956. "That is his right to die."

A momentous shift was taking place during the postwar era, but so gradually and invisibly that, like the shift of tectonic plates deep underground, one would realize it only years later when the earthquake happened. Americans began focusing on both sides of the doctor-patient relationship: not only the physician's choice of treatment but his patient's experience. Unlike their nineteenth-century ancestors, however, they did not define "a good death" as a blessing. They defined it as a right. In keeping with the equal-rights movement developing among blacks and the due-process rights being asserted by courts for alleged criminals, Americans increasingly advocated the right to die. Legally speaking, that had no meaning. Nor did it have meaning in common sense. As one commentator has sardonically remarked, "I'd prefer to give up my right to die."

The Right to Die

For years Americans were uncertain, unclear, or simply inconsistent about what they were calling for. Not the right to kill oneself. More typically, especially before 1950, they were referring to a doctor hastening death with or without the patient's consent. Sometime they had in mind suicide with the assistance of a physician. In the fifties and sixties they also focused on what Judge Baldwin in 1899 had prophetically called a "natural death"—namely, the withholding or withdrawal of extraordinary life-prolonging treatment. Americans defined "the right to die" in one or another of these ways, or sometimes left it undefined, but with growing intensity they asserted a claim to a good death.

The voices gradually swelled into a public chorus. "To prolong life uselessly . . . ," a professor of theology wrote in 1954, "is to attack the moral stratus of a person." "As physicians," wrote an eminent psychiatrist in 1962, "we must recognize the dignity of man and his right to live and die peacefully." "Should a new right—the right to die—be added to the triad of 'inalienable rights' to life, liberty and the pursuit of happiness?" a journalist wondered in 1966. "No one can be against 'dying with dignity,'" declared the editors of an influential Catholic journal. In 1974 ABC television produced an hour-long documentary titled "The Flight to Die," a U.S. Senate committee held three days of hearings on "Death with Dignity," and a group of lawyers, doctors, and philosophers gathered at Agnes Scott College for a weekend symposium on death and dying. Even more telling, the Euthanasia Society of America was resurrected by a new set of leaders under a new name, the Society for the Right to Die. Where it had once advocated the active hastening of death, it now argued for the right to forgo or end life-support and promoted the use of living wills.

But the earthquake—the event that reshaped the cultural landscape by giving irrevocable meanings and force to "the right to die"—occurred only in 1975. That was when Joseph and Julia Quinlan went to court in New Jersey, asking that their comatose daughter be taken off a respirator.

Euthanasia Should Be Legalized

Derek Humphry

Active euthanasia refers to the personal decision to end one's own life to relieve suffering. In the majority of situations, individuals choose euthanasia as a result of a painful and terminal disease. In the following selection, pro-euthanasia activist and author Derek Humphry discusses the benefits of legalizing active euthanasia and physician-assisted suicide. He reports that several organizations are committed to legalizing euthanasia in the United States to help people increase personal control when faced with a painful and hopeless terminal disease. He notes that hospice care is not an answer for every patient because not everyone responds to pain control medications. Humphry also suggests that everyone should protect themselves by creating living wills and durable powers of attorney so that they will have control over their death if they become incapacitated and end-of-life decisions fall to others. He concludes by asserting that the right to die in a manner of one's choosing is the ultimate civil liberty.

When active voluntary euthanasia becomes lawful . . . it is not something every dying person will want or need. Yet getting legal help with a dying process unbearable to the patient will be a comfort to a good many sufferers, and will relieve prosecution worries for those physicians who today perform the act covertly.

Moreover, legalizing the right to choose to die will have two additional benefits: First, it will provide comforting assurance to those who would want this right in the future if they were suffering. Countless thousands, even though they would prefer a doctor's help, have stored or wish to store lethal amounts of drugs because they fear a bad death.

Second, legalization will lengthen the life for many. From my position as executive director of the Hemlock Society [a right to die organization, now renamed], I observe numerous suicides of people who, lacking such legal means, end their lives early because they fear the loss of control later on.

Personal Experience

People often ask me how I came into this rather unusual movement and how I've lasted twelve years. I had no knowledge or interest in euthanasia until one day my first wife, Jean, asked me to help her die. She was suffering from breast cancer that had metastasized into her bones. She and I both knew her death was only a matter of time.

I saw the logic of her request and agreed to secure a lethal potion of drugs with which she could end her life at a time chosen by her. She was insistent that she would pick the time; in fact, she had a remission and hung on for a further nine months.

But in March 1975, when she was critically ill and very debilitated, her doctors gently informed her that there was nothing left they could do. Jean discharged herself from the hospital, and three days later asked me for the drugs. After we had spent several hours saying our last goodbyes, she drank a cup of coffee containing the drugs—which a sympathetic doctor illicitly had supplied—and died peacefully.

Without fully realizing the consequences, I published a little book called *Jean's Way*, in 1978. The book's worldwide publication, plus the ensuing debate that it triggered, made me a well-known proponent of euthanasia. I knew my action in helping Jean die was illegal, but fortunately, the London public prosecutor who had ordered an inquiry when the book appeared, realized from the evidence that Jean was the prime mover in her suicide. I was not prosecuted.

Even after I moved to the United States and became a writer for the *Los Angeles Times*, the subject of euthanasia would not go away. People kept asking me to do something about it. . . . So in 1980, I formed the Hemlock Society to educate the public through books, newsletters, and public speeches, and to set the scene for the legal reform on euthanasia that is going to be a major battleground in the 1990s. As with abortion rights, the right to choose to die is a so-called "pro-choice" controversy. Abortion and the right to die differ in that the mother is deciding for the unborn fetus, while in euthanasia, individuals decide for themselves—a much stronger argument. . . .

The Netherlands is the only country in the world that has given the green light to euthanasia. Since a 1984 Dutch Supreme Court case, physicians there are allowed to give a lethal injection to a dying patient who makes a clear and consistent request.

Most politicians are leery of this issue at present, and members of the Dutch parliament are no exception. It is still a crime when a physician in the Netherlands helps a person to die, but the physician need not fear prosecution so long as the criteria laid down by the Supreme Court are followed.

In Britain, where the euthanasia society now called EXIT was founded back in 1935, a supportive parliamentary lobby is building, and a sixth legislative attempt is not far off. Across the world, thirty societies in twenty countries promote the idea of lawful assisted suicide for the dying. There are four societies in Australia, two in Belgium, one in Spain and one group in India.

Reasons for Euthanasia

In the twelve years I have been involved in this cause, I find two principal reasons for euthanasia that are constantly evidenced by polls in numerous countries:

One. Public dread of dying while connected to sophisticated life-support equipment, which creates loss of personal control over one's life, a drain on family finances, or both.

Two. People demanding the choice to make up their own minds because easily understandable public information on medical matters is now readily available in print, on radio, and on television.

Why, some ask, is euthanasia necessary when good pain management through careful use of drugs is available to almost everybody in developed countries? I have listened to many medical voices on pain control, and they summarize the situation as being able to control the pain of terminal illness in about 90 percent of cases. This means that if you take the statistic that three thousand people die every day in the United States, then about three hundred people meet their end while suffering. Also, what makes one person's life happy and bearable is different from another's. Inability to read would be unendurable to some, but inconsequential to others, and so on. Then there are the factors of distress, personal indignities, and the psychic pain of death. Loss of bowel control, indigestion, itching, and numerous other disorders may be minor to the physician, but excruciating to the patient.

Legal Debate

In the United States, the debate on the right to die has reached all the way to the Supreme Court for the first time. The parents of Nancy Cruzan, whose brain was damaged severely in a car accident [in 1983] are seeking permission to have their daughter disconnected from her life-support system. If permission is granted . . . , the tubes that supply her with nutrition and hydration will be disconnected, and over the next few weeks she will starve to death. [After a three-year court battle that ended in the U.S. Supreme Court, Cruzan's feeding tube was removed in December of 1990.]

With cases like Nancy Cruzan's, we are talking about what is known as "passive euthanasia" —allowing someone to die by disconnecting life-support equipment. If Nancy had signed a Living Will, she could have been allowed to die within a few months of her car accident because, in effect, she would have signed a "release."

Fifty states of the United States have legalized Living Wills [in 2006], and millions of Americans have signed them. There is another useful document available under U.S. law—the Durable Power of Attorney for Health Care. With this piece of paper, you can assign someone else to make medical decisions for you should you become incompetent. This authority can include disconnection of life-support equipment, but it does not include permission to actively end your life.

The Hemlock Society recommends that everybody sign these documents to protect themselves to the fullest extent the law allows, but also feels that there should be another form of escape from suffering available: active voluntary euthanasia— helping a patient to die through physician-assisted suicide.

Until this becomes law, people who want release from terminal suffering must practice what is known as "self-deliverance." To assist in doing this properly, Hemlock has for nine years published a book, *Let Me Die Before I Wake*. The book gives instructions on how to end one's own life, including a section telling how not to get loved ones into legal trouble.

But Hemlock looks forward to the day when it can scrap its suicide manual. We hope patients will have access to lawful aid-in-dying from physicians, on very clearly defined terms, and with appropriate safeguards against abuse. For me and many others, the right to die in a manner of one's own choosing is the ultimate civil liberty.

Euthanasia Should Not Be Legalized

Andrew Fergusson

Legalization of euthanasia continues to be a hotly debated topic in the twenty-first century. In this selection, physician Andrew Fergusson, a Christian and an Englishman, examines the issue through the lens of personal experience. He briefly considers the arguments for legalizing euthanasia and then refutes these arguments by countering them with Christian ethics. He concludes that there is no right to euthanasia and that physicians should focus on providing a gentle and easy environment until patients' naturally occurring death.

J was a patient of mine in general practice. He had been action man personified in work and sport, but several years of progressive multiple sclerosis with no remissions had left him almost tetraplegic. He was well looked after, with maximum nursing and homecare input, and despite no specific treatment several hospital specialists supervised his management. I visited regularly for support.

After a couple of years, J suddenly asked, 'Doc, go out to your car, get something, and put me out of this. If I was an animal, you'd have to.' For a moment, my heart agreed with him, but then a lot of other realisations kicked in. 'J', I said, and I was so glad to be able to say this, 'that's against the law and I'm not going to do it. And you know I'm a Christian and what you've just said gives me a particular problem. But I'm glad you've raised it, because I hadn't realised how bad things had got, and I promise that from now on we're going to work twice as hard for you.'

And we did. Even so, J made the same request monthly for about two years. You will conclude I never performed eutha-

Andrew Fergusson, "Why We Shouldn't Legalise Euthanasia," *Nucleus*, April 2005, pp. 13–18. Copyright © 2005 Christian Medical Fellowship. Reproduced by permission.

nasia, although the story didn't end there. But first, this story illustrates well the focus of the current debate. . . .

Three Arguments for Euthanasia

All medics need to know the arguments for and against legalising euthanasia. There are essentially three arguments for:

* We want it—the autonomy argument
* We need it—the compassion argument
* We can control it—the public policy argument . . .

The Christian Case

The Christian case against euthanasia can be stated very briefly. No Scripture can be found in favour and the sixth Commandment, 'You shall not murder', which prohibits the intentional killing of the legally innocent applies. But as J's story illustrates, most of us will meet situations where we ask ourselves, however momentarily, 'Why does God say that?'

Christians should support autonomy in so far as it reflects the unique value of each human being made 'in the image of God' but autonomy is not absolute. I will now major on four arguments against the autonomy case for euthanasia, and conclude with brief reflections only on the other two arguments. These answers go some way towards explaining the 'No' an infinitely wise and loving God has clearly given us; because they are essentially secular they do this in ways that a non-Christian public can understand and identify with.

Four Objections From Autonomy

1) Following the patient's autonomy impacts the doctor's. Where a patient's autonomy is followed so far that they receive a prescription for lethal medication or are put to death at the end of a needle, the doctor's autonomy is compromised. The euthanasia lobby reply, 'So what? There is a Conscience Clause in Lord Joffe's Bill. Objectors need not be involved.' But we know the Conscience Clause in [England's] 1967 Abortion Act has only worked partially, and abortion has kept many doctors away from obstetrics/gynaecology and general practice.

While you can avoid abortion as a doctor and still have career choice, there is no branch of medicine where you can entirely avoid issues of death and dying. What impact might euthanasia legislation have on recruitment and retention of staff in all medical specialties? Manpower is an ever-growing difficulty for the [English] National Health Service.

2) Most patients have 'another question'. Those who care for the dying know the (relatively few) who currently ask for euthanasia usually have another question behind their question. This may be physical—a distressing symptom needs treating; psychosocial—they want honesty within their family; or spiritual—they have questions like 'Why me?' or 'Why now?'

There is an old medical adage: 'No treatment without a diagnosis'. If we bother to make a real diagnosis and then treat that, the request for euthanasia usually goes away. Prescribing euthanasia, even with the proposed safeguards, would far more often undermine autonomy than underline it.

3) But there are deliberated requests! Why can't they have euthanasia? J's requests were deliberated. Why with controls can't there be a law to accommodate exceptional cases? The answer is a development of the previous point. For the reasons hinted at there, and bearing in mind inevitable uncertainty about prognosis, to change the law to allow euthanasia for this small minority within a minority would mean it was performed far more often when it was 'wrong' than when some would see it as 'right'. To protect that majority, the minority forego a right that doesn't exist anyway.

This sounds utilitarian but it has to be so in complex inter-connected societies. In road traffic legislation for example, we all accept limitations on our 'freedoms' in order to protect vulnerable others. John Donne's famous words 'no man is an island' hint at the issues of community and relationships central to the euthanasia debate. Respect for the right of autonomy has to be balanced with the responsibilities that accept restrictions.

4) Allowing 'voluntary' euthanasia won't end there. 'Slippery slopes' exist. If we change the law to allow voluntary euthanasia for those who are suffering and have the capacity to ask for it, surely compassion means we should similarly provide euthanasia for that patient who is suffering at least as much but has no capacity to request it? This logical slippery slope follows when doctors decide that any patient's life is not worth living (the euthanasia lobby argue the patient decides—but the doctor has to agree).

There are other slippery slopes, in practice and in doctors' attitudes. The progression from voluntary to non-voluntary euthanasia (the patient lacks capacity) or involuntary euthanasia (a patient with capacity is not consulted) is well documented in the Netherlands.

The Remmelink Report was a statistically valid analysis of all 129,000 deaths in the Netherlands in 1990: 3% were euthanasia. Of that 3%, 1 in 3, 1% of all deaths in the Netherlands in 1990, were euthanasia 'without explicit request'. In 1990 Dutch doctors killed more than 1,000 patients without their request. This is not patient autonomy but doctor paternalism of the worst kind.

We Need It—The Compassion Argument

Briefly, this stands or falls on the answer to the question: Do we have to kill the patient to kill the symptoms? Palliative care has answered that question with a resounding 'No', though the harder symptoms to deal with are not positive physical ones but negative ones of patients' losses—the things they can't do any more. The challenge to healthcare becomes bringing meaning and hope in the face of suffering.

We Can Control It—The Public Policy Argument

As the Dutch statistics confirm, we cannot control it. How ever could we, when the key witness, the person police would most want to interview, is dead?

Of course, another way to exercise some control over euthanasia would be to require doctors to notify cases to the authorities so that checks could subsequently be made. Such a situation was in force in the Netherlands in 1990, as one of the so-called 'strict safeguards'. According to Remmelink there should therefore have been 3,700 notifications in 1990 (3,300 cases of euthanasia and a further 400 of physician assisted suicide). How many notifications were there? There were 454.

In the vast majority of cases doctors chose to conceal what they had done, in the process perjuring themselves on death certificates and other legally binding documents. The euthanasia movement has argued that the doctors were only trying to spare relatives the distress of legal enquiries on top of their grief, but how do we know that was always the case? Perhaps some of those doctors had something to hide.

The reporting rate has been checked several times since then but the rate in 2001 was still only 54%. Even since the complete legalisation of euthanasia in 2002 (in 1990 it was only 'legally sanctioned'), numbers of reported cases have continued to fall. This has prompted the Dutch health minister to order a follow up study in 2005.

The 'We can control it' claim does not work, and hence the public policy argument fails too.

There is no 'right' to be killed by a doctor, we do not need euthanasia, and we could never control it. All three arguments are tried and found wanting. Let us instead commit ourselves to working for that genuinely 'gentle and easy death' all our patients deserve.

Expanded Hospice Care Is a Better Alternative to Euthanasia

David Cundiff

The debate between those who are for and those who are against euthanasia and physician-assisted suicide is often couched in terms of moral absolutes. The individual, inalienable right to decide when to die is set against the sanctity of life. In the following selection, hospice care physician David Cundiff suggests that if proper end of life care is available, there should be no need for euthanasia or physician-assisted suicide, thus ending the moral contest. He proposes basic changes in the U.S. health care system that would encourage the founding of hospice programs offering good pain control and caring facilities. Cundiff concludes that terminally ill patients can live out their final days in comfort and with the love and support of friends and family rather than ending their life prematurely through euthanasia or assisted suicide.

The word "euthanasia" comes from a Greek phrase meaning "good death." In today's society it means killing a terminally ill person as a way to end that person's pain and suffering. Unfortunately, most people equate terminal cancer or AIDS with constant, unrelieved pain and suffering. Fortunately, today's medicine can greatly alleviate the pain and suffering from these and other diseases in all dying people. But it is also regrettably true that the majority of physicians in the United States have never been taught the techniques of treating the physical, psychological, and emotional symptoms of terminal disease. . . .

Assisting suicide means to provide a person who plans to kill himself with the means to do so. This may be accomplished by supplying a lethal overdose of medication, by providing a gun, or by other means. . . .

Allowing a Terminally Ill Person to Die Naturally

Euthanasia or "active euthanasia" is often confused with allowing the terminally ill person to die naturally of the disease. Allowing an individual to die means foregoing or stopping medical treatments intended to prolong life. For example, a terminally ill person on a respirator (breathing machine) in an intensive care ward may request that the machine be turned off and that he or she be allowed to die. The discontinuation of life support technology when any realistic hope for recovery has completely vanished is a legal, ethical, and appropriate act also known as passive euthanasia.

A poor substitute term for "allowing to die," "passive euthanasia" implies that there is a strong similarity with active euthanasia. Proponents of active euthanasia argue that the difference between passive and active euthanasia is little more than semantic. But though it is simple, the difference is much more than that. In one case, the person dies naturally of the disease process, whereas in the other, the person is killed by the injection of an overdose of medication. The US courts and medical associations also make this critical distinction. . . .

People with cancer, AIDS, or other medical conditions are always legally free to choose whether to have particular medical treatments. No one is obligated by law to accept intravenous hydration, antibiotics for infections, renal dialysis (kidney machine) treatments for kidney failure, or other medical therapies if these would only prolong needless suffering. At some point such measures become useless in every patient with advanced incurable cancer or AIDS. For many terminally ill people, life-prolonging treatments can all too easily become a fate worse than death. And sad as it may seem, nature should be allowed to take its course at some point. . . .

Traditionally, death with dignity has meant that the dying are kept physically comfortable and given psychological, emotional, and spiritual support by skilled medical professionals in conjunction with their caring families and loved ones. Meddlesome and unnecessary diagnostic procedures and therapies should be avoided and, if possible, the dying should live their last days in their own homes in their own beds. Personally, I would hardly consider it 'death with dignity' if the pain and other physical and psychological symptoms of my own terminally ill patients were so out of control that they were begging for euthanasia or assisted suicide. . . .

Hospice or Palliative Care

The hospice approach to the treatment of the terminally ill focuses on relieving the physical symptoms of patients and on providing psychological and social support for both patient and family. Whereas standard medical treatment for cancer and AIDS patients strives to prolong life at virtually any cost, hospice seeks to optimize the quality of life of the patient's remaining time. The National Hospice Organization defines the hospice philosophy as:

> Hospice affirms life. Hospice exists to provide support and care for persons in the last phases of incurable disease so that they might live as fully and comfortably as possible. Hospice recognizes dying as a normal process whether or not resulting from disease. Hospice neither hastens nor postpones death. Hospice exists in the hope and belief that, through appropriate care and the promotion of a caring community sensitive to their needs, patients and families may be free to attain a degree of mental and spiritual preparation for death that is satisfactory to them.

Palliative care is a synonym for hospice.

With notable, exceptions, hospice or palliative care services in the United States are woefully inadequate. Improved training in hospice for all medical professionals and the allocation of a greater proportion of cancer and AIDS treatment resources to hospice care are urgently needed.

Who Wants Euthanasia and Why Would One Want It?

Informal polls among cancer specialists show that requests for euthanasia or assisted suicide are very uncommon. Two of my oncologist colleagues with more than 25 years of combined experience reported that only two of their patients had ever asked for euthanasia or assisted suicide. The published literature confirms my impression about the rarity of euthanasia requests despite the frequency of poorly treated physical and psychological symptoms.

Why do some terminally ill people want euthanasia or assisted suicide? By all accounts terminally ill people wanting euthanasia or suicide cite *pain* as the chief factor driving them to end their lives.

I have treated several thousand cancer and AIDS patients in the past 18 years, first as a medical oncologist (cancer treatment specialist), and then as a palliative care doctor. Ten of my patients have asked for euthanasia. Another 15 or 20 attempted suicide. Only three that I know about actually succeeded in committing suicide.

In my experience the cases in which terminally ill people either requested euthanasia or committed suicide are similar. Poor pain control, other physical symptoms out of control, or inadequate psychosocial support occur invariably. Cases from the literature in which detailed information is provided confirm this impression.

Tragically, in the vast majority of these cases, the pain could have been readily alleviated and other physical symp-

toms suffered by these patients could have been better controlled if the caregivers had expertise in palliative care techniques. More appropriate psychological, social, and spiritual
support might well have been provided if the physicians,
nurses, and other health care workers were adequately trained.

It is a disgrace that the majority of our health care providers lack the knowledge and the skills to treat pain and other
symptoms of terminal disease properly. The absence of palliative care training for medical professionals results in subopti-
mal care for almost all terminally ill patients and elicits the
wish to hasten their own deaths in a few. . . .

English Versus American Health Care Systems

Ironically, the socialized medicine environment in England
seems to foster good cancer pain control and overall palliative
care. The reasons for this are complex, involving the superior
training of English physicians in palliative care, the more realistic expectations of the English public concerning medical
technology, and incentives in the English medical system fa-
voring palliative care. As a result of the interplay of all these
factors, English general practitioners and oncologists (cancer
specialists) refer terminally ill cancer and AIDS patients to
hospice programs much earlier in the disease process than do
U.S. physicians.

All of this is made possible because hospice training is
more readily available in England than in the United States.
English physicians and nurses may enroll in numerous hospice training programs to learn about pain and symptom
management. As a consequence of freely available hospice
training, experts in hospice are much more available and hospital and community resources for hospice treatment are part
of standard care in England.

The American medical system—or patchwork of systems—
unintentionally fosters barriers to optimal pain and symptom

management for terminally ill people. Lack of physician and nurse training in palliative care is a major barrier previously discussed.

Ironically, financial disincentives also discourage good pain and symptom control for doctors and for hospitals. Patients with poorly controlled pain and other symptoms fill empty hospital beds and require many more costly physician services. A good measure of the effectiveness and quality of palliative care services is the degree of success in managing the patient's symptoms at home so that only minimal time in the hospital is necessary. Consequently, the better the palliative care provided, the more money the doctor and hospital lose compared to standard oncology care.

Medical care reform needs to address the perverse disincentives that often obstruct good pain and symptom control. Increased reimbursement for Medicare and Medicaid hospice benefits tops the list of reforms needed to improve health care in America. . .

Better Palliative Care—The Alternative to Euthanasia

The unnecessary physical and mental torment of dying in a standard medical setting can be incredible. However, with excellent palliative care, the dying process can instead be associated with profound emotional and spiritual growth for the patients, as well as for the loved ones and caregivers.

Ideally, the debate surrounding the legalization of euthanasia should center around the inadequacies of palliative care in this country, but this has not been the case. Neither the pro-euthanasia nor the anti-euthanasia forces have sufficiently highlighted the inadequacies of palliative care training or the meager medical resources directed toward hospice. Nor has either camp offered tangible proposals for alleviating the unnecessary suffering of the terminally ill.

Hospice should be at the top of the agenda for health care reform in this country. Improved hospice services can simultaneously improve the quality of care and reduce its cost. Increased access to medical care services naturally follows the discovery of a low-cost, high-quality alternative therapy.

Education of the public about these issues is necessary to effect change. One hopes that the controversy so strongly stirred by the state euthanasia initiatives will stimulate concerned citizens to learn much more about hospice. With increased public awareness, leaders in the health care field will follow. Action by American legislators, insurance companies, medical administrators, health educators, and other concerned citizens is essential if the hospice approach is to grow, and thus produce a dramatic improvement in the treatment of cancer patients.

Reactions to the Legalization of Physician-Assisted Suicide in Oregon

Derek Humphry and Mary Clement

In 1997, physician-assisted suicide was made legal in Oregon. The law permits competent, terminally ill adults to have their assisted suicide request considered by a physician. The legislated assisted suicide process is detailed and requires an assessment of the medical facts including the patient's state of depression, health status, diagnosis, and exploration of other options. In this selection, pro-euthanasia activist Derek Humphry and attorney Mary Clement discuss the scope of the Oregon law and the ethical debate surrounding its enactment. The law met with mixed reception. The right to die movement's hopes for national legalized euthanasia and physician-assisted suicide were bolstered. Conversely, the U.S Catholic Conference of Bishops were horrified and called the law a tragedy for seriously ill patients.

History was made in Oregon in 1997 when its citizens became the first community to confirm by popular vote the legalization of PAS [Physician-Assisted Suicide] for the terminally ill. Through a political miscalculation by its opponents, this was the second vote within three years on an identical law by the same electorate. On the first occasion the law passed by a mere 2 percent margin, but the second time around it succeeded by 20 percent. A more thorough and democratic demonstration of the public will could hardly have been deliberately orchestrated; the fault lay with opponents, who, overzealous in their desire to destroy the 1994 law, ended up greatly increasing the mandate for its implementation. . . .

A Limited Legalization

The law passed in Oregon was not as broad as that permanently sanctioned in the Netherlands since 1984, or that which operated in the Northern Territory of Australia for nine months in 1996–97. It was a law tailored both for the shortcomings in the American health insurance system, and the puritanical streak that permeates a good deal of American morality. While the two other countries simultaneously introduced both active voluntary euthanasia (death by injection) and PAS (death by taking lethal drugs prescribed by a doctor), Oregon chose PAS alone as the best hope of getting a law onto the statute books. Ballot initiatives introducing both methods of assisted dying had previously failed in Washington State (1991) and in California (1992), each getting 46 percent of the popular vote.

What the Oregon law permits is for a terminally ill adult, close to death, who has made a competent and consistent request for drugs with which to kill him- or herself, to have that request considered by a doctor. Before that can happen there are many precautions against mistakes, hastiness, or abuse, such as a fifteen-day waiting period, a second opinion by another doctor, investigation of whether pain control is adequate, and assessment of possible depression. Provided members of the medical staff obey the law meticulously, they are free from criminal prosecution and administrative or professional punishment. A "conscience clause" allows health professionals and hospitals to decline to participate in a hastened death; the patient must then seek an alternate doctor. Any coercion, forgery, or fraud resulting in an untimely death is punishable as a serious felony. This law, unique in the United States, first took effect on October 27, 1997. It was the end of a seventeen-year struggle to legalize a concept, and the start of a drive to make it available across the country.

A Mixed Reaction to the New Law

Predictably, reception to the Oregon result was mixed. Dr. Peter Goodwin, a Portland internal medicine physician who had been a fighter for law reform for many years, commented: "It's a huge step forward for the care of the dying, and a powerful message to the rest of the country. Legislatures throughout the country are going to have to look at this vote and realize that if this is what the people are saying, we better respond more positively than we have in the past."

The U.S. Catholic Conference of Bishops issued a statement calling the vote "a tragedy for seriously ill patients who deserve better care for their real needs, not an invitation to suicide." Boston's Cardinal Law weighed in with the oft-repeated warning that "a right to die" easily becomes a "duty to die" once society labels some lives as not worth living.

Public response could be gauged by the impassioned letters to the editors of newspapers. A man in Tualatin wrote: "The winning side believed in the best of the judgment of individuals and their caretakers. The losers were trying to convince us that doctors were at best incompetent and at worst evil, and we as individuals are completely unable to take care of ourselves ... We are a society of intelligent and well-meaning citizens, not idiots or kids." A reader from Eugene complained: "Our beautiful state will now be known as the 'death state' and being old, ill and living in Oregon will be detrimental to one's life." The *Eugene Register-Guard*, the second biggest paper in the state, which had long supported PAS, rejoiced under a headline GOOD SENSE ON SUICIDE: "The majority, including ourselves, see assisted suicide as a rational choice that ought to be accessible to the dying. The availability of the choice, not the desirability of suicide, is the crux of the matter—just as with abortion." The state's largest newspaper, *The Oregonian*, which had furiously resisted both ballot measures, moaned in an editorial entitled "The abyss": "With their reaffirmation of the state's 1994 assisted suicide law, Oregonians have officially surrendered the state's sole authority to use lethal force, and turned a small part of that power over to a profession—doctors. No other government in the world has gone so far. That's our idea of an abyss." But the people had spoken through the democratic process, and, despite some rear-guard actions by opponents, the law went into effect, slowly and cautiously, as a divided medical profession considered its newly appointed responsibility.

CHAPTER 3

Reproductive Technology and Cloning

Chapter Preface

Lesley Brown was unable to become pregnant due to a physical condition that prevented her eggs from traveling from her ovaries into the fallopian tubes and uterus, where fertilization takes place. Prior to 1977, Lesley and her husband, John, had only one major option to have a child together—adoption. However, on November 10, 1977, Lesley Brown underwent a procedure conducted by Dr. Patrick Steptoe and Dr. Robert Edwards that removed eggs directly from her ovaries, mixed them with her husband's sperm in a test tube, and then placed the resulting fertilized egg into Lesley's uterus. This procedure, called in vitro fertilization (IVF), allowed Lesley to become pregnant and resulted in the birth of the first "test tube baby," Louise Brown, on July 25, 1978. Advances in reproductive technology allowed couples like the Browns to have biological children but have also stimulated ethical debate over the use of technology to create children outside of a mother's womb.

In the 1970s, the possible future applications of reproductive technology, like IVF, captured society's imagination and led to public fears of rooms of babies in test tubes created by science and not through human contact. Individuals such as Dr. James D. Watson, one of the discoverers of the structure of the DNA molecule, called for an international multidisciplinary group of scientists, ethicists, and politicians to debate and regulate the uses of future reproductive technologies. Watson voiced his hopes that "over the next decade wide-reaching discussion would occur, at the informal as well as formal legislative level, about the manifold problems which are bound to arise if test-tube conception becomes a common occurrence." Although some discussion and debate did occur around reproductive technologies, no related legislation was passed in the 1970s. In addition, as IVF became a widespread and accepted medical procedure, fears over reproductive technologies dwindled.

In 1997, however, the birth of Dolly, the first genetically cloned sheep, symbolized the next advance in reproductive technologies and restimulated ethical, legal, social, and political debate. Cloning is a procedure that uses the genetic information from an adult cell to create an identical twin, or copy, of an organism by inserting the adult nucleus into an egg from which the nucleus has been removed. The resulting embryo is then implanted into the uterus of a surrogate mother. The ability to clone a sheep suggested that scientists could soon use cloning as a way to produce human children that were genetically identical to their parents. Just like in the 1970s, the idea raised fears concerning the unethical use of technology to create "unnatural children."

Fierce debate continues to rage in 2006 about the ethical implications of the different types of reproductive technology. Some groups feel that using technologies to produce babies violates the sanctity of life. Their concerns about reproductive technologies focus on issues related to "playing God" and interfering with the natural order of life. Opponents assert that some technologies such as therapeutic and reproductive cloning should be allowed to continue because cloning may be useful in treating or preventing disease as well as assisting infertile couples in becoming parents. The selections found in the following chapter provide historical background on reproductive technology and the cloning debate while highlighting major bioethical perspectives on these issues.

The First Test Tube Baby Raises Ethical Issues

National Review

On July 25, 1978, Louise Brown, the first baby conceived through the use of in vitro fertilization (IVF), was born in England. The following selection by the staff of the conservative magazine National Review *discusses the ethical debate stimulated by the use of the technology to produce a human baby. They report that theologians and moralists were split in their views of the implications of test tube babies. Other commentary was mostly positive except for individuals who felt that manipulation of the egg and sperm exposes test tube babies to unknown risks and decreases reverence for life. The* National Review *submits that as technology alters the ability of humans to reach into unexplored territories, the motivations and purpose behind such advances should be examined as much as the use of the technology.*

On July 25, at Oldham General and District Hospital in Lancashire, England, a female baby weighing 5 pounds 12 ounces and named Louise Brown was delivered by Caesarean techniques, her mother being Lesley Brown, wife of a truck driver. The only unusual feature of the baby's biography to date is the fact that the ovum had been fertilized in the laboratory and then implanted in Mrs. Brown.

The Religious Reaction

Theologians, clergymen, and moralists exhibited considerable disarray. A spokesman for the New York Archdiocese described the means of conception as "morally objectionable." In Rome, a Vatican official said that "Fecundation must be carried out according to nature. . . ." According to a priest at the Archdiocese of Brooklyn, "the natural act must take place." However, these statements by no means reflect Catholic unanimity, other priests and theologians made diverse comments, often favorable, and both Protestant and Jewish spokesmen tended to be favorable, from a variety of moral and theological perspectives.

The Lay Commentary

Lay comment tended to be mostly favorable, though with notable exceptions. Catholic ethical thinker Daniel Callaghan thought the fertilized and developing egg had been subjected to unknown risks, and George Will raised the question of the disposal of surplus eggs and even embryos, as well as other issues, and concluded that "Some manipulation of life must, over time, subvert our sense of mystery, and so our reverence for life."

Techniques and Technology Stimulate Ethical Debate

No doubt the techniques used to bring Louise Brown into existence raise a thicket of ethical and theological problems as well as technological and political choices, but the entire matter also raises, so to speak, a generic problem, having to do with the fact of modernity.

[Early nineteenth-century German philosopher Georg] Hegel argued a hundred years ago, in his *Philosophy of History* that all of human history is moving inexorably toward freedom, the possibilities of action ever expanding in all realms of advanced culture. Hegel appears to have been right.

Without raising knotty problems of philosophy, it appears true to say that the definition of "nature" frequently appealed to by Catholic spokesmen seems at least tacitly to ignore the fact that "mind" is a component of nature, and has the capacity constantly to transform it.

For this reason, the area in which conscious choices must be made enlarges dynamically. Should we engage in genetic engineering if, for example, cancer might be eliminated by doing so? Maybe not, but mind is rendering such engineering a possibility very much within "nature." Should we colonize space? Maybe not, but we are free to do so. Organ transplants, life-support systems: choice. Everywhere limits retreat, collapse. This expansion of human possibility appears to be relentless and irreversible. At some point, as Hegel foresaw, the only necessity may be freedom.

To be sure, as the area of choice expands, so do the possibilities of good and evil. Therefore the quality of the motive involved becomes constantly more important, especially as it becomes more difficult to understand a "dynamic" nature as in some way normative. Under these circumstances it may be St. Paul, not some version of "natural law," who speaks most directly to an age when men are moving into space, walking on the moon, penetrating genetic secrets, harnessing the sun-like fusion reaction: "I may speak in tongues of men or of angels, but if I am without love, I am a sounding gong or a clanging cymbal. . . . Put love first."

As for Louise Brown, welcome aboard Space Ship Earth. It is going to be quite a journey from here on out.

New Reproductive Technologies Require International Policy Regulations

James D. Watson

Prior to the birth of Louise Brown, the first test tube baby, and Dolly, the first cloned sheep, the co-discoverer of DNA, James D. Watson called for ethical discussion over use of future reproductive technologies. In the following selection written in 1971, Watson argues that international policy should be established before cloning and other reproductive technologies become a reality. He emphasizes that the desire to use new reproductive technologies to allow infertile couples to have their own biological babies and the drive of scientists to expand their knowledge will cause the rapid adoption of technologies once they are available. He recognizes the difficulty of international consensus, but concludes that if nations don't address the issue now, the ability to make a reasoned choice about reproductive technologies will be taken away by the unstoppable progress of science.

The notion that man might sometime soon be reproduced asexually upsets many people. The main public effect of the remarkable clonal frog produced some ten years ago in Oxford by the zoologist John Gurdon has not been awe of the elegant scientific implication of this frog's existence, but fear that a similar experiment might someday be done with human cells. Until recently, however, this foreboding has seemed more like a science fiction scenario than a real problem which the human race has to live with. . . .

James D. Watson, "Moving Toward the Clonal Man," *The Atlantic*, May 1971, pp. 50–53. Reproduced by permission of the author.

Technology is Progressing Quickly

Today, however, we must face up to the fact that the unexpectedly rapid progress of R.G. Edwards and P.S. Steptoe in working out the conditions for routine test-tube conception of human eggs means that human embryological development need no longer be a process shrouded in secrecy. It can become instead an event wide-open to a variety of experimental manipulations. Already the two scientists have developed many embryos to the eight-cell stage, and a few more into blastocysts, the stage where successful implantation into a human uterus should not be too difficult to achieve. In fact, Edwards and Steptoe hope to accomplish implantation and subsequent growth into a normal baby within the coming year. . . .

Some very hard decisions may soon be upon us. It is not obvious, for example, that the vague potential of abhorrent misuse should weigh more strongly than the unhappiness which thousands of married couples feel when they are unable to have their own children. Different societies are likely to view the matter differently, and it would be surprising if all should come to the same conclusion. We must, therefore, assume that techniques for the *in vitro* manipulation of human eggs are likely to become general medical practice, capable of routine performance in many major countries within some ten to twenty years.

The situation would then be ripe for extensive efforts, either legal or illegal, at human cloning. But for such experiments to be successful, techniques would have to be developed which allow the insertion of adult diploid nuclei into human eggs which previously have had their maternal haploid nucleus removed. At first sight, this task is a very tall order since human eggs are much smaller than those of frogs, the only vertebrates which have so far been cloned. Insertion by micropipettes, the device used in the case of the frog, is always likely to damage human eggs irreversibly. Recently, however, the development of simple techniques for fusing animal cells has raised the strong possibility that further refinements of the cell-fusion method will allow the routine introduction of human diploid nuclei into enucleated human eggs. Activation of such eggs to divide to become blastocysts, followed by implantation into suitable uteri, should lead to the development of healthy fetuses, and subsequent normal-appearing babies.

The growing up to adulthood of these first clonal humans could be a very startling event, a fact already appreciated by many magazine editors, one of whom commissioned a cover with multiple copies of Ringo Starr, another of whom gave us overblown multiple likenesses of the current sex goddess, Raquel Welch. It takes little imagination to perceive that different people will have highly different fantasies, some perhaps imagining the existence of countless people with the features of Picasso or Frank Sinatra or Walt Frazier or Doris Day. And would monarchs like the Shah of Iran, knowing they might never be able to have a normal male heir, consider the possibility of having a son whose genetic constitution would be identical to their own?. . .

Predicted Reactions to Human Clones

The first reaction of most people to the arrival of these asexually produced children, I suspect, would be one of despair. The nature of the bond between parents and their children, not to mention everyone's values about the individual's uniqueness, could be changed beyond recognition, and by a science which they never understood but which until recently appeared to provide more good than harm. Certainly to many people, particularly those with strong religious backgrounds, our most sensible course of action would be to de-emphasize all those forms of research which would circumvent the normal sexual reproductive process. If this step were taken, experiments on cell fusion might no longer be supported by federal funds or tax-exempt organizations. Prohibition of such research would most certainly put off the day when diploid nuclei could satisfactorily be inserted into enucleated human eggs. Even more effective would be to take steps quickly to make illegal, or to reaffirm the illegality of, any experimental work with human embryos.

Neither of the prohibitions, however, is likely to take place. In the first place, the cell-fusion technique now offers one of the best avenues for understanding the genetic basis of cancer. Today, all over the world, cancer cells are being fused with normal cells to pinpoint those specific chromosomes responsible for given forms of cancer. In addition, fusion techniques are the basis of many genetic efforts to unravel the biochemistry of diseases like cystic fibrosis or multiple sclerosis. Any attempts now to stop such work using the argument that cloning represents a greater threat than a disease like cancer is likely to be considered irresponsible by virtually anyone able to understand the matter.

Though more people would initially go along with a prohibition of work on human embryos, many may have a change of heart when they ponder the mess which the population explosion poses. The current projections are so horrendous that responsible people are likely to consider the need for more basic embryological facts much more relevant to our self-interest than the not-very-immediate threat of a few clonal men existing some decades ahead. And the potentially militant lobby of infertile couples who see test-tube conception as their only route to the joys of raising children of their own making would carry even more weight. So, scientists like Edwards are likely to get a go-ahead signal even if, almost perversely, the immediate consequences of their "population-money"-supported research will be the production of still more babies.

A Call for International Cloning Policy

Complicating any effort at effective legislative guidance is the multiplicity of places where work like Edwards' could occur, thereby making unlikely the possibility that such manipulations would have the same legal (or illegal) status throughout the world. We must assume that if Edwards and Steptoe produce a really workable method for restoring fertility, large numbers of women will search out those places where it is legal (or possible), just as now they search out places where abortions can be easily obtained.

Thus, all nations formulating policies to handle the implications of *in vitro* human embryo experimentation must realize that the problem is essentially an international one. Even if one or more countries should stop such research, their action could effectively be neutralized by the response of a neighboring country. This most disconcerting impotence also holds for the United States. If our congressional representatives, upon learning where the matter now stands, should decide that they want none of it and pass very strict laws against human embryo experimentation, their action would not seriously set back the current scientific and medical momentum which brings us close to the possibility of surrogate mothers, if not human clonal reproduction. This is because the relevant experiments are being done not in the United States, but largely in England. That is partly a matter of chance, but also a consequence of the advanced state of English cell biology, which in certain areas is far more adventurous and imaginative than its American counterpart. There is no American university which has the strength in experimental embryology that Oxford possesses.

We must not assume, however, that today the important decisions lie only before the British government. Very soon we must anticipate that a number of biologists and clinicians of other countries, sensing the potential excitement, will move into this area of science. So even if the current English effort were stifled, similar experimentation could soon begin elsewhere. Thus it appears to me most desirable that as many people as possible be informed about the new ways of human reproduction and their potential consequences, both good and bad.

This is a matter far too important to be left solely in the hands of the scientific and medical communities. The belief that surrogate mothers and clonal babies are inevitable because science always moves forward, an attitude expressed to me recently by a scientific colleague, represents a form of laissez-faire nonsense dismally reminiscent of the creed that American business, if left to itself, will solve everybody's problems. Just as the success of a corporate body in making money need not set the human condition ahead, neither does every scientific advance automatically make our lives more "meaningful." No doubt the person whose experimental skill will eventually bring forth a clonal baby will be given wide notoriety. But the child who grows up knowing that the world wants another Picasso may view his creator in a different light.

I would thus hope that over the next decade wide-reaching discussion would occur, at the informal as well as formal legislative level, about the manifold problems which are bound to arise if test-tube conception becomes a common occurrence. A blanket declaration of the worldwide illegality of human cloning might be one result of a serious effort to ask the world in which direction it wished to move. Admittedly the vast effort, required for even the most limited international arrangement, will turn off some people—those who believe the matter is of marginal importance now, and that it is a red herring designed to take our minds off our callous attitudes toward war, poverty, and racial prejudice. But if we do not think about it now, the possibility of our having a free choice will one day suddenly be gone.

The First Cloned Sheep Prompts Debate on the Ethics of Human Cloning

Clarisa Long and Christopher DeMuth

In 1997, Dr. Ian Wilmut in Edinburg, Scotland, led a research team that oversaw the birth of the first cloned sheep, Dolly. The announcement escalated ethical and policy debate both inside and outside scientific and medical circles. The surge in discussion was less in response to the successful cloning of an animal than to the notion that the new technology would soon result in human cloning. In response to the looming idea of human cloning, the United States government moved quickly and halted any human cloning attempts using federal funds until the ethical and legal issues had been reviewed. As Clarisa Long and Christopher DeMuth explain in the following selection, the official responsibility for reviewing the issues surrounding human cloning fell to the National Bioethics Advisory Commission (NBAC). After discussing the ethical, legal, and social implications of human cloning, the NBAC reported that cloning technology continues to raise serious ethical concerns that needed to be addressed prior to the use of the technology to clone humans. Long and DeMuth also report that the media and the public have expressed fears over cloning. The authors note, however, that such hesitancy will not likely stop or impede the advance of cloning technology. Christopher DeMuth is an attorney, former professor of public policy, and president of the American Enterprise Institute, a conservative policy organization. Clarisa Long is an attorney and professor at the University of Virginia School of Law. Prior to

Clarisa Long and Christopher DeMuth, "Introduction" to *The Ethics of Human Cloning*. Washington, D.C.: The AEI Press, 1998, pp. vii–xxi. Copyright © 1998 by the American Enterprise Institute for Public Policy Research, Washington, D.C. All rights reserved. Reproduced by permission.

joining the faculty of the University of Virginia, she taught at Harvard University's Kennedy School of Government, and was the Abramson Fellow at the American Enterprise Institute.

In 1971 James D. Watson, codiscoverer with Francis Crick of the double-helical structure of DNA, predicted that one day human cloning would be possible and urged that "as many people as possible be informed about the new ways for human reproduction and their potential consequences, both good and bad." Watson's prediction seemed far-fetched at the time, and his admonition was ignored. In the subsequent quarter-century, genetics became a booming, rapidly progressing science. Along with prodigious advances in our knowledge of biological nature and many tangible improvements in medical diagnostics and practice, molecular biology generated a series of discrete ethical and policy issues. Does genetic research present public health hazards? Should genetically engineered molecules, tissues, and animals be patentable? Should individuals have a "right to privacy" concerning genetic information (such as predisposition to disease)? Yet the prospect of cloning whole animals, and *Homo sapiens* himself, remained remote, and the ethical implications of such an astounding development went largely unexplored.

That all changed on February 23, 1997, with the news that Dolly the lamb had been cloned from the nonreproductive tissue of one adult female sheep so that she was genetically identical to her sole progenitor. The news was called "extraordinary," "stupendous," "mind-boggling," "frightening," and even "the scientific discovery of the century." Suddenly, Dr. Ian Wilmut, head of the research team at the Roslin Institute in Edinburgh, Scotland, where the cloning took place, went from being an obscure embryologist to the focus of media attention and investor interest. Dolly became a celebrity, the butt of countless jokes, a symbol of modern science, and a source of hype and even hysteria. Most of the commentary, however, was concerned not with Dolly herself or with Dr. Wilmut's scientific discovery, but rather with the specter of human cloning and its implications for human welfare. . . .

Why Dolly Is Different

Dolly grew from a sheep embryo that had been created not in the usual way—from a female egg joining with a male sperm to produce a genetically mixed offspring—but rather from an egg that had been implanted with the full complement of genetic material from a second (female) sheep. . . .

The genetic manipulation that produced Dolly is colloquially called "cloning." Cloning, however, is a general term, describing any procedure that produces a precise genetic replica of a biological object, including a DNA sequence, a cell, or an organism. Scientists have been cloning elementary substances such as genes and cells for years; today, much routine biological research and many important pharmaceutical applications depend on that sort of cloning, which involves few of the ethical dilemmas presented by the cloning of human beings and higher animals. . . .

Social and Political Responses to Dolly

The first effect of the Dolly announcement was to fire the public imagination. Commentators were quick to speculate about the possibility of cloning a human. The *Los Angeles Times* opined that such a discovery "opens the door to a 'Blade Runner' world of human replicants." No less sober a publication than the *Wall Street Journal* asked business leaders and newsmakers whether they would like to have themselves cloned. Feminists observed that the technique finally made men superfluous. Tabloid newspapers warned of "master races" and promised production lines of movie and sports stars.

Government reaction to the news was swift. President [William] Clinton ordered that no federal funds be spent on human cloning (as far as anyone knows, none had been) and directed the National Bioethics Advisory Commission (NBAC) to "conduct a thorough review of the legal and the ethical issues raised" by human cloning.

The NBAC issued its report, *Cloning Human Beings*, on June 9, 1997. The commission's main conclusion was unequivocal: "At this time it is morally unacceptable for anyone in the public or private sector, whether in a research or clinical setting, to attempt to create a child using somatic cell nuclear transfer cloning." The commission's consensus on that point was based on safety—that is, that using somatic cell [non-reproductive] nuclear transfer for the purpose of creating a child entailed significant uncertainties and "unacceptable risks to the fetus and/or potential child"—but it also emphasized that "many other serious ethical concerns have been identified, which require much more widespread and careful public deliberation before this technology may be used." At the same time, the commission recognized that somatic cell nuclear transfer technology may have many beneficial applications for biotechnology, livestock production, and new medical applications, including the production of pharmaceutical proteins and prospects for regeneration and repair of human tissues, and it noted that it is "notoriously difficult to draft legislation at any particular moment that can serve to both exploit and govern the rapid and unpredictable advances of science."

The NBAC made the following five recommendations. First, the president's moratorium on the use of federal funds to support any attempt to create a child by somatic cell nuclear transfer should be continued, and all firms, clinicians, investigators, and professional societies should be requested to comply voluntarily with the intent of the federal moratorium. Second, federal legislation should be enacted to prohibit anyone from attempting, whether in a research or clinical setting, to create a child through somatic cell nuclear transfer. Third, the United States should cooperate with other countries to enforce mutually supported restrictions on human cloning.

Fourth, any regulatory or legislative actions undertaken to effect a prohibition on human cloning should be carefully written so as not to interfere with other important areas of research, such as the cloning of human DNA sequences and cells. Finally, cloning animals by somatic cell nuclear transfer should be subject only to existing regulations regarding the humane use of animals, since the technique does not raise the same issues implicated in attempting to use it to create a child.

Following release of the NBAC report, President Clinton endorsed legislation to prohibit for five years the use of somatic cell nuclear transfer cloning to create a human being and to continue the ban on the use of federal funds for research leading to human cloning. In 1997 and 1998 numerous bills to ban human cloning were introduced in the U.S. Congress. Most were similar to the version endorsed by the president—banning (temporarily or indefinitely) any effort to use somatic cell nuclear transfer to clone a human being, protecting other forms of genetic research (including the cloning of nonhuman animals), and calling for further study and reports by the NBAC and other bodies.

The scientists, ethicists, religious leaders, and business executives testifying before Congress in hearings on those bills were in general agreement about human cloning. In his testimony before the Senate, Dr. Wilmut said that human cloning would be "unethical" and "quite inhumane." James Geraghty, president of Genzyme Transgenics Corporation, testified that the biotechnology industry overwhelmingly agreed that there is no legitimate reason in our society to clone human beings and stated that biotechnology firms are well aware of the need to operate within socially accepted norms of behavior. Scientists and biotechnology executives were equally insistent, however, that any legal restriction on human cloning avoid interfering with beneficial applications of cloning technologies, such as to produce genetically identical research animals for improving the speed and accuracy of pharmaceutical research. And many witnesses emphasized the numerous uncertainties concerning somatic cell nuclear transfer and the distant prospects of human cloning. Thomas H. Murray of the Center for Biomedical Ethics, for example, emphasized in his testimony before the House of Representatives that "good ethics begins with good facts" and proceeded to describe many of the biological conundrums [surrounding the issue].

[As of 2006, no] national legislation concerning human cloning has been enacted in the United States. (Some restrictions have been enacted [in some individual States] and in Europe.) But no one doubts that the political debate will continue and intensify—perhaps prompted by further, currently unanticipated scientific developments—and that the likelihood of some form of legislative response is strong.

Fictional Representations of Technology Influence the Cloning Debate

Matthew Nisbet

Before cloning was proved to be possible in animals or humans, fictional representations sculpted the cultural view of reproductive technologies. Books like Frankenstein, The Boys from Brazil, *and* Brave New World *portrayed cloning in a negative light and embodied the fear and distaste felt for genetic manipulation. In this selection, Ohio State University assistant professor Matthew Nisbet ponders the intersection of science, media, and politics found in portrayals of cloning in literature, movies, and media. He focuses on the power of these fictional representations to impact current political debate and policy making.*

Consider the following plot summary [from George Lucas's film *Star Wars, Episode II: Attack of the Clones*], compiled from credible reports on the Web:

> Leaders of the Republic, a loosely democratic coalition of intergalactic planets, find themselves faced with the threat of insurrection and terrorist assassinations. In this situation, they are manipulated by the power hungry Senator Palpatine to acquiesce in the development, by cloning, of a million-man storm-trooper army, which will battle the rebels and serve as muscle for the few hundred noble Jedi knights.

> The clones, genetically identical copies of a skilled bounty hunter named Jango Fett, are subjected to growth acceleration, programmed to be obedient, and mass produced into 20-year old super soldiers. Fett vainly adopts one clone as

his own son, a self-replica named Boba, who Fett allows to grow at a normal rate, keeping the child in constant tow under his close tutelage. Although the clones are created for the "greater good" of the Republic, and eventually prove their worth in battle, menacing dilemmas are foreshadowed for the third installment of the prequel series. (Internet rumors speculate that in the third film, the clones come under the control of Palpatine and are used to hunt down and kill the Jedi, bringing Palpatine to power.)

If all this sounds familiar, that's because it's straight out of *The Boys from Brazil* or *Brave New World*, with a touch of *Frankenstein* thrown in. Channeling these classic texts, the latest *Star Wars* film presents an array of motifs that pop up again and again in public discussions about the societal impact of science, and powerfully structure our perceptions of live-wire political issues like cloning. Indeed, as University College London historian of science John Turney writes in his book *Frankenstein's Footsteps: Science, Genetics and Popular Culture*, "fictional representations matter . . . the science and technology we ultimately see are partly shaped by the images of the work which exist outside the confines of the laboratory report or the scientific paper."

A recent example of this occurred when Leon Kass, head of President Bush's Council on Bioethics, assigned his fellow council members an 1843 Nathaniel Hawthorne story called "The Birthmark" to help structure their thoughts about issues like stem-cell research. Meanwhile, the conservative *Weekly Standard*'s William Kristol, generally fond of the *Brave New World* analogy, has already titled one of his anti-cloning commentaries "Attack of the Clones." It may sound absurd, but we must seriously ask the question: Like *Frankenstein* and *Brave New World*, what impact could *Star Wars* have on the human-cloning controversy in this country?

The Second Wave of Cloning Debate

Much like *Attack of the Clones* itself, the present cloning debate is really "Episode Two" of a heated political battle that began with [2001's] struggle over funding for human embryonic stem-cell research. Indeed, the rhetoric and imagery from popular culture wielded in the current dispute over two competing bills in the Senate—the Brownback-Landrieu bill to ban both reproductive and "therapeutic cloning" (a term used to describe the process of embryo replication for research purposes) and the Feinstein-Kennedy legislation to ban cloning only for reproductive purposes—evolved during the 2001 stem-cell controversy.

[The 2001] stem-cell debate was easily linked to issues of genetic engineering and cloning, evoking vivid images from culture and history. The relationship was not lost on various interests in opposition to research, whose talking points frequently included references to "playing God," Dr. Frankenstein, a "brave new world," Faustian bargains, and the Nazi holocaust, as well as menacing adjectives such as "evil," "murderous," and "gruesome." Journalists, often attracted to drama and familiar storytelling themes and captivated by a narrative that could be told in terms of conflict and controversy, maximized these popular culture references in news accounts. Their reporting featured the technical expertise of scientists, but pitted scientific views against those of pro-life and religious interests.

Media Portrayal of Cloning Increases Debate

The media's ability to dramatize coverage of the stem-cell controversy helps explain why the issue received so much attention in 2001. According to a recent study that we conducted at Cornell University, although stem-cell research had been ongoing for four decades, the media virtually ignored it until 2001, when the issue could be fit into a dramatic, conflict-oriented context. Our analysis finds that in association with a sharp rise in media attention, the use of dramatic storytelling themes also increased markedly, with a quarter of all stem-cell-related articles in 2001 featuring some reference to science fiction, popular culture, or historical metaphor. Moreover, the media framed coverage predominantly in terms of political strategy and conflict. This structuring of discourse by competing political actors and journalists so as to emphasize popular fiction, drama, and conflict continues with the 2002 debate over cloning legislation—and suggests an obvious opening for the megacultural phenomenon that is *Star Wars* to have a serious impact.

After all, the groundwork has been well laid by reporters. Consider the opening to an April 14 *Milwaukee Journal-Sentinel* news article by staff writer Marilyn Marchione: "In the brave new world of biotechnology, few things are as primally frightening as the prospect of humans being churned out of laboratories like widgets from factories." Or the opening penned by staff writer Tom Abate for a February 25 *San Francisco Chronicle* article detailing a recent scientific meeting: "Designer babies, bionic adults and genetically 'improved' humans used to be the stuff of science fiction, but now these are not merely possible but probable outcomes of biotechnology." (The headline writer added more literary allusion to the article with the tag: "Brave new world of genetics explored at Academy of Sciences meeting.")

Literary Cloning References Direct the Focus of Discussions

Finally, consider a May 5 *New York Times* Week-in-Review article by veteran science writer Sheryl Gay Stolberg, headlined "It's Alive! It's Alive!" Stolberg interviewed a number of scientists and research proponents who were perplexed by the emphasis on the "mad scientist" threat in cloning research. "Popular culture is replete with scientific cautionary tales:

Frankenstein and Dr. Strangelove, to name two," she wrote. "And history has witnessed science put to evil purpose: the Nazi experiments on Jews, biowarfare and the atomic bomb. But does that necessarily mean science itself is to be feared?" Stolberg asked rhetorically.

Opponents of cloning research know very well that journalists are drawn to these dramatic literary conventions in formulating news accounts. They also know that many of these popular culture and historical metaphors frame biotechnology issues in ways that favor their preferred policy outcomes. By discussing cloning and biotech research in terms of *Frankenstein*, mad scientists, or *Brave New World*, cloning opponents emphasize certain dimensions of the issue over others, limiting debate to terms that marshal support for their position.

This tactic is most readily apparent in a number of paid political advertisements that have been running [in 2002] in Washington, D.C., and in the home states of senators viewed as swing votes on the cloning legislation (or who may be vulnerable on pro-life wedge issues come the November elections). In these radio and television spots, the pro-life groups emphasize themes of mass commodification, manufacture, and mass harvesting—all of which pop up in *Attack of the Clones*. Take this radio ad sponsored by the National Right to Life Committee (NRLC) that began running in Arkansas last week, with key metaphors and frames in italics:

ANNOUNCER: A message from Arkansas and National Right to Life.

WOMAN: Honey, look at this story. It looks like Senator Blanche Lincoln will probably vote to allow human embryos to be cloned and then killed in experiments.

MAN: What?

WOMAN: Remember President Bush urged the Senate to pass the Brownback bill to ban human cloning, before human *"embryo farms"* open for *business* in this country? Well, some *biotech corporations* really want to clone human embryos, grow them for a while, then *kill them for their parts*. But Blanche Lincoln apparently thinks that's OK—as long as they fill out some paperwork and make sure all the embryos die while they are still small.

MAN: Let me see that. Lincoln Sees Pluses In Cloning Embryos? My word! But look here—at least our other senator, Tim Hutchinson, supports the Brownback ban that President Bush wants. Hutchinson said that cloning is *"human beings trying to take the role of God."*

WOMAN: Well, he's right. *It's wrong to create human embryos and then harvest them like crops.*

ANNOUNCER: If you agree with President Bush and Senator Hutchinson that the cloning of human embryos should be banned, then urge Senator Lincoln to join them in support of the Brownback bill.

These NLRC ads come on the heels of other radio and television spots that have been on the airwaves since March. These earlier ads, sponsored by Stop Human Cloning, a group chaired by the aforementioned William Kristol, targeted four undecided Democratic senators in Georgia and North Dakota and played on similar themes. Kristol was up front about Stop Human Cloning's message strategy in comments to the *Washington Post* back on March 5. "With these ads we're taking the debate to the American people," Kristol said, "and we're confident that they will urge their senators to close this door leading to the horrors of the Brave New World."

Scientists Bemoan Fictional Terminology

So has public discourse on cloning gravitated towards the Dark Side? Scientists certainly seem to think so. Researchers have long lamented the use of the term "cloning" to describe the technical procedure they prefer to call "somatic nuclear transfer." For example, in a February 15 editorial in the journal *Science*, prominent scientists Bert Vogelstein, Bruce Alberts, and Kenneth Shine wrote that "The goal of creating a nearly identical genetic copy of a human being is consistent with the term human reproductive cloning, but the goal of creating stem cells for regenerative medicine is not consistent with the term therapeutic cloning." The trio continued: "Although it may have been conceived as a simple term to help lay people distinguish two different applications of somatic cell nuclear transfer, 'therapeutic cloning' is conceptually inaccurate and misleading, and should be abandoned."

But though the term "cloning" may be technically misapplied in this context, there is little that scientists can do to shift the current nature of debate, or disassociate "therapeutic cloning" from *Star Wars*-esque interpretations. Instead, therapeutic cloning advocates would be better off adopting message strategies that promote their own preferred policy outcomes, as they have indeed begun to do. In congressional testimony and in op-eds, for example, scientist Paul Berg and former Senator Connie Mack have compared the hyperbolic metaphors applied by cloning opponents to similar rhetoric used in opposition to recombinant DNA research during the 1970s. As Mack and Berg argue, despite the harsh claims of opponents, Congress eventually allowed rDNA research to continue, leading to significant advances in biotechnology with no known calamities or disasters.

Although the current message strategies used both by opponents and proponents of cloning research might fall short of certain notions of ideal democratic discourse, they play on the realities of the political arena. The public and lawmakers alike draw upon popular culture, including the moral lessons of *Frankenstein, Brave New World*, and even *Star Wars*, as heuristics for making up their minds about cloning. Although *Star Wars* allusions have thus far been relatively few and far between in the cloning debate, we can expect them to pick up. . . . After all, to the victors in this war of literary allusion and colorful metaphor go the political spoils.

All Human Cloning Should be Banned

George W. Bush

In July 2001, the United States House of Representatives voted to make all experiments involving human cloning a criminal offense. The banned procedures included reproductive cloning and cloning to create an embryo for derivation of stem cells for therapeutic research. Since then, cloning legislation has stalled in the Senate where support for certain types of non-reproductive therapeutic cloning prevents any cloning ban from being passed. Accordingly, the United States has not passed into law any ban on cloning. In a nationally televised address on April 10, 2002, of which a transcript follows, U.S. president George W. Bush stated his position that all forms of cloning should be banned and emphasized his support for the legislative banning of human cloning. Bush endorsed the house bill banning all human cloning, stating that cloning would likely result in the genetic engineering of children to custom specifications. The ability to change children would make them a commodity rather than a natural creation, Bush argued. He also opposed therapeutic (or research) cloning because it would require the creation and destruction of human embryos and because the direct benefits of research cloning cannot be proved. Bush also noted that anything other than a total ban on human cloning would be virtually impossible to enforce.

All of us here today believe in the promise of modern medicine. We're hopeful about where science may take us. And we're also here because we believe in the principles of ethical medicine.

George W. Bush, "President Bush Calls on Senate to Back Human Cloning Ban," April 2002, www.whitehouse.gov.

As we seek to improve human life, we must always preserve human dignity. And therefore, we must prevent human cloning by stopping it before it starts. . . .

A Time for Restraint

We live in a time of tremendous medical progress. A little more than a year ago, scientists first cracked the human genetic code—one of the most important advances in scientific history. Already, scientists are developing new diagnostic tools so that each of us can know our risk of disease and act to prevent them.

One day soon, precise therapies will be custom made for our own genetic makeup. We're on the threshold of historic breakthroughs against AIDS and Alzheimer's Disease and cancer and diabetes and heart disease and Parkinson's Disease. And that's incredibly positive.

Our age may be known to history as the age of genetic medicine, a time when many of the most feared illnesses were overcome.

Our age must also be defined by the care and restraint and responsibility with which we take up these new scientific powers.

Advances in biomedical technology must never come at the expense of human conscience.

As we seek what is possible, we must always ask what is right, and we must not forget that even the most noble ends do not justify any means.

Science has set before us decisions of immense consequence. We can pursue medical research with a clear sense of moral purpose or we can travel without an ethical compass into a world we could live to regret. Science now presses forward the issue of human cloning. How we answer the question of human cloning will place us on one path or the other.

Human cloning is the laboratory production of individuals who are genetically identical to another human being.

Cloning is achieved by putting the genetic material from a donor into a woman's egg, which has had its nucleus removed. As a result, the new or cloned embryo is an identical copy of only the donor. Human cloning has moved from science fiction into science.

One biotech company has already begun producing embryonic human clones for research purposes. Chinese scientists have derived stem cells from cloned embryos created by combining human DNA and rabbit eggs. Others have announced plans to produce cloned children, despite the fact that laboratory cloning of animals has lead to spontaneous abortions and terrible, terrible abnormalities.

Life Is Not a Commodity

Human cloning is deeply troubling to me, and to most Americans. Life is a creation, not a commodity. Our children are gifts to be loved and protected, not products to be designed and manufactured. Allowing cloning would be taking a significant step toward a society in which human beings are grown for spare body parts, and children are engineered to custom specifications; and that's not acceptable.

In the current debate over human cloning, two terms are being used: reproductive cloning and research cloning. Reproductive cloning involves creating a cloned embryo and implanting it into a woman with the goal of creating a child. Fortunately, nearly every American agrees that this practice should be banned. Research cloning, on the other hand, involves the creation of cloned human embryos which are then destroyed to derive stem cells.

I believe all human cloning is wrong, and both forms of cloning ought to be banned, for the following reasons. First, anything other than a total ban on human cloning would be unethical. Research cloning would contradict the most fundamental principle of medical ethics, that no human life should be exploited or extinguished for the benefit of another.

Yet a law permitting research cloning, while forbidding the birth of a cloned child, would require the destruction of nascent human life. Secondly, anything other than a total ban on human cloning would be virtually impossible to enforce. Cloned human embryos created for research would be widely available in laboratories and embryo farms. Once cloned embryos were available, implantation would take place. Even the tightest regulations and strict policing would not prevent or detect the birth of cloned babies.

Third, the benefits of research cloning are highly speculative. Advocates of research cloning argue that stem cells obtained from cloned embryos would be injected into a genetically identical individual without risk of tissue rejection. But there is evidence, based on animal studies, that cells derived from cloned embryos may indeed be rejected.

Yet even if research cloning were medically effective, every person who wanted to benefit would need an embryonic clone of his or her own, to provide the designer tissues. This would create a massive national market for eggs and egg donors, and exploitation of women's bodies that we cannot and must not allow.

Alternative Means of Making Progress

I stand firm in my opposition to human cloning. And at the same time, we will pursue other promising and ethical ways to relieve suffering through biotechnology. This year for the first time, federal dollars will go towards supporting human embryonic stem cell research consistent with the ethical guidelines I announced [in] August [2001].

The National Institutes of Health [NIH] is also funding a broad range of animal and human adult stem cell research. Adult stem cells which do not require the destruction of human embryos and which yield tissues which can be transplanted without rejection are more versatile than originally thought.

We're making progress. We're learning more about them. And therapies developed from adult stem cells are already helping suffering people.

I support increasing the research budget of the NIH, and I ask Congress to join me in that support. And at the same time, I strongly support a comprehensive law against all human cloning. And I endorse the bill—wholeheartedly endorse the bill—sponsored by Senator Brownback and Senator Mary Landrieu.

This carefully drafted bill would ban all human cloning in the United States, including the cloning of embryos for research. It is nearly identical to the bipartisan legislation that last year passed the House of Representatives by more than a 100-vote margin. It has wide support across the political spectrum, liberals and conservatives support it, religious people and nonreligious people support it. Those who are pro-choice and those who are pro-life support the bill.

This is a diverse coalition, united by a commitment to prevent the cloning and exploitation of human beings. It would be a mistake for the United States Senate to allow any kind of human cloning to come out of that chamber.

I'm an incurable optimist about the future of our country. I know we can achieve great things. We can make the world more peaceful, we can become a more compassionate nation. We can push the limits of medical science. I truly believe that we're going to bring hope and healing to countless lives across the country. And as we do, I will insist that we always maintain the highest of ethical standards.

Therapeutic Cloning Should Not Be Banned

Michael J. Sandel

The following selection began as a lecture delivered by Harvard professor and philosopher Michael Sandel in 2003 at an international conference on cloning. In this paper, Sandel presents his argument that therapeutic cloning for the production of stem cells is ethical and should be allowed to continue while reproductive cloning should be banned. Sandel notes that human cloning aimed at creating designer babies is the ultimate expression of human pride. The process of selective enhancement of certain features detracts from the natural miracle that produces children. He argues that therapeutic research cloning, by contrast, has merit because it may provide treatment options for patients with debilitating diseases. Sandel concludes that he supports therapeutic cloning within the context of moral restraint and oversight of embryo research by national committees.

Much of the debate about cloning and genetic engineering is conducted in the familiar language of autonomy, consent, and individual rights. Defenders of "liberal eugenics" [the use of genetic engineering to improve humans] argue that parents should be free to enhance the genetic traits of their children for the sake of improving their life prospects. [American philosopher] Ronald Dworkin, for example argues that there is nothing wrong with the ambition "to make the lives of future generations of human beings longer and more full of talent and hence achievement." In fact, he maintains, the principle of ethical individualism makes such efforts obligatory. Many opponents of cloning and genetic engineering also invoke the language of autonomy and rights. For ex-

Michael J. Sandel, "The Ethical Implications of Human Cloning," *Jahrbuch fur Wissenschaft und Ethick 8*, 2003, pp. 241–247. Reproduced by permission of the author.

ample [German philosopher, sociologist, and political scientist] Jurgen Habermas worries that even favorable genetic enhancements may impair the autonomy and individuality of children by pointing them toward particular life choices, hence violating their right to choose their life plans for themselves.

But talk of autonomy and rights does not address the deepest questions posed by cloning. In order to grapple with the ethical implications of cloning and genetic engineering, we need to confront questions largely lost from view in the modern world—questions about the moral status of nature and about the proper stance of human beings toward the given world. Since questions such as these verge on theology, or at least involve a certain view of the best way for human beings to live their lives, modern philosophers and political theorists tend to shrink from them. But our new powers of biotechnology make these questions unavoidable.

In the United States today, no federal law prohibits human cloning, either for purposes of reproduction or for purposes of biomedical research. This is not because most people favor reproductive cloning. To the contrary, public opinion and almost all elected officials oppose it. But there is strong disagreement about whether to permit cloning for biomedical research. And the opponents of cloning for biomedical research have so far been unwilling to support a separate ban on reproductive cloning, as Britain has enacted. Because of this stalemate, no federal ban on cloning has been enacted. . . .

The Flaws of Current Moral Views

I turn now to the ethics of cloning for biomedical research. It is here that the greatest disagreement prevails. The U.S. Senate is split between those who want to ban all cloning and those who want to ban reproductive cloning but not cloning for stem cell research and regenerative medicine. As in the case of reproductive cloning, the concepts of autonomy and rights cannot by themselves resolve the moral question. In order to assess the moral permissibility of cloning for stem cell research, we need to determine the moral status of the early embryo. If the six-day, pre-implantation embryo (or blastocyst) is morally equivalent to a person, then it is wrong to extract stem cells from it, even for the sake of curing devastating diseases such as Parkinson's, Alzheimer's, or diabetes. If the embryo is a person, then not only should all therapeutic cloning be banned, so also should all embryonic stem cell research.

Before turning to the moral status of the embryo, I would like to consider one influential argument against cloning for biomedical research that stops short of opposing embryonic stem cell research as such. Some opponents of research cloning, troubled by the deliberate creation of embryos for research, support embryonic stem cell research, provided it uses "spare" embryos left over from fertility clinics. Since in vitro fertilization (IVF) clinics (at least in the United States) create many more fertilized eggs than are ultimately implanted, some argue that there is nothing wrong with using those spares for research: if excess embryos would be discarded anyway, why not use them (with donor consent) for potentially life-saving research?

This seems to be a sensible distinction. But on closer examination, it does not hold up. The distinction fails because it begs the question whether the "spare" embryos should be created in the first place. If it is immoral to create and sacrifice embryos for the sake of curing or treating devastating diseases, why isn't it also objectionable to create and discard spare IVF embryos in the course of treating infertility? Or, to look at the argument from the opposite end, if the creation and sacrifice of embryos in IVF is morally acceptable, why isn't the creation and sacrifice of embryos for stem cell research also acceptable? After all, both practices serve worthy ends, and curing diseases such as Parkinson's, is at least as important as enabling infertile couples to have genetically related children.

Judgments on Embryo Research Must Stand or Fall Together

Of course, bioethics is not only about ends, but also about means. Those who oppose creating embryos for research argue that doing so is exploitative and fails to accord embryos the respect they are due. But the same argument could be made against fertility treatments that create excess embryos bound for destruction. In fact, a recent study found that some 400,000 frozen embryos are languishing in American fertility clinics, with another 52,000 in the United Kingdom and 71,000 in Australia.

If my argument is correct, it shows only that stem cell research on IVF spares and on embryos created for research (whether natural or cloned) are morally on a par. This conclusion can be accepted by people who hold very different views about the moral status of the embryo. If cloning for stem cell research violates the respect the embryo is due, then so does stem cell research on IVF spares, and so does any version of IVF that creates and discards excess embryos. If, morally speaking, these practices stand or fall together, it remains to ask whether they stand or fall. And that depends on the moral status of the embryo.

The Moral Status of the Embryo

There are three possible ways of conceiving the moral status of the embryo: as a thing, as a person, or as something in between. To regard an embryo as a mere thing, open to any use we may desire or devise, is, it seems to me, to miss its significance as nascent human life. One need not regard an embryo as a full human person in order to believe that it is due a certain respect. Personhood is not the only warrant for respect: we consider it a failure of respect when a thoughtless hiker carves his initials in an ancient sequoia, not because we regard the sequoia as a person, but because we consider it a natural wonder worthy of appreciation and awe—modes of regard inconsistent with treating it as a billboard or defacing it for the sake of petty vanity. To respect the old growth forest does not mean that no tree may ever be felled or harvested for human purposes. Respecting the forest may be consistent with using it. But the purposes should be weighty and appropriate to the wondrous nature of the thing.

One way to oppose a degrading, objectifying stance toward nascent human life is to attribute full personhood to the embryo. I will call this the "equal moral status" view. One way of assessing this view is to play out its full implications, in order to assess their plausibility. Consider the following hypothetical: a fire breaks out in a fertility clinic, and you have time to save either a five-year-old girl or a tray of 10 embryos. Would it be wrong to save the girl?

A further implication of the equal moral status view is that harvesting stem cells from a six-day-old blastocyst is as morally abhorrent as harvesting organs from a baby. But is it? If so, the penalty provided in the proposed U.S. anti-cloning legislation—a $1 million fine and 10 years in prison—is woefully inadequate. If embryonic stem cell research is morally equivalent to yanking organs from babies, it should be treated as a grisly form of murder, and the scientist who performs it should face life imprisonment or the death penalty.

A further source of difficulty for the equal moral status view lies in the fact that, in natural pregnancies, at least half of all embryos either fail to implant or are otherwise lost. It might be replied that a high rate of infant mortality does not justify infanticide. But the way we respond to the natural loss of embryos or even early miscarriages suggests that we do not regard these events as the moral or religious equivalent of infant mortality. Otherwise, wouldn't we carry out the same burial rituals for the loss of an embryo that we observe for the death of a child?

The conviction that the embryo is a person derives support not only from certain religious doctrines but also from the . . . assumption that the moral universe is divided in binary terms: everything is either a person, worthy of respect, or a thing, open to use. But this dualism is overdrawn.

Proceed with Reverence

The way to combat the instrumentalizing impulse of modern technology and commerce is not to insist on an all-or-nothing ethic of respect for persons that consigns the rest of life to a utilitarian calculus. Such an ethic risks turning every moral question into a battle over the bounds of personhood. We would do better to cultivate a more expansive appreciation of life as a gift that commands our reverence and restricts our use. Human cloning to create designer babies is the ultimate expression of the hubris that marks the loss of reverence for life as a gift. But stem cell research to cure debilitating disease, using six-day-old blastocysts, cloned or uncloned, is a noble exercise of our human ingenuity to promote healing and to play our part in repairing the given world.

Those who warn of slippery slopes, embryo farms, and the commodification of ova and zygotes are right to worry but wrong to assume that cloning for biomedical research necessarily opens us to these dangers. Rather than ban stem cell cloning and other forms of embryo research, we should allow it to proceed subject to regulations that embody the moral restraint appropriate to the mystery of the first stirrings of human life. Such regulations should include licensing requirements for embryo research projects and fertility clinics, restrictions on the commodification of eggs and sperm, and measures to prevent proprietary interests from monopolizing access to stem cell lines. This approach, it seems to me, offers the best hope of avoiding the wanton use of nascent human life and making these biomedical advances a blessing for health rather than an episode in the erosion of our human sensibilities.

All Forms of Human Cloning Are Ethical

Alex Epstein

In the following article Alex Epstein argues that therapeutic and reproductive cloning are medical breakthroughs worth celebrating. In his view, embryos are not human beings and the use of stem cells from cloned human embryos is ethical because the patients receiving the benefits of stem cell therapies are humans in need. Similarly, reproductive cloning is ethical because it involves applying medical advances to the betterment of humanity. Epstein asserts that past celebrated medical achievements—such as vaccinations and in vitro fertilization—have had their detractors as well. Epstein states that to ban cloning because of blind fear would be ignorant and immoral. Alex Epstein is a writer for the Ayn Rand Institute, the stated goal of which is to spread objectivism, the belief that all reality is objective and external to the mind and that knowledge is reliably based on observed fact.

In a huge breakthrough for medical progress, scientists from South Korea have finally created a cloned human embryo and extracted its stem cells—a feat that makes life-saving embryonic stem-cell treatments that much closer to reality [the cloning report was later shown to be a fraud]. Instead of taking this thrilling news as an opportunity to celebrate cloning, politicians and intellectuals are once again calling for bans. Some seek to ban all cloning, while others oppose "only" reproductive cloning. Although each group claims the moral high ground, both positions are profoundly *immoral*. Any attempt to ban human cloning technology should be rejected permanently, because cloning—therapeutic *and* reproductive—is morally good.

Therapeutic Cloning Is Ethical

Consider first therapeutic cloning, which opponents perversely condemn as "anti-life." Senator Sam Brownback [R-KS], who has sponsored a Congressional ban on all cloning, says therapeutic cloning is "creating human life to destroy [it]." President [George W.] Bush calls it "growing human beings for spare body parts."

In fact, therapeutic cloning is a highly *pro*-life technology, since cloned embryos can be used to extract medically potent embryonic stem cells. A cloned embryo is created by inserting the nucleus of a human body cell into a denucleated egg, which is then induced to divide until it reaches the embryo stage. These embryos are not human beings, but microscopic bits of protoplasm the width of a human hair. They have the *potential* to grow into human beings, but *actual* human beings are the ones dying for lack of this technology. The embryonic stem cells extracted from a cloned embryo can become any other type of human cell. In the future, they may be used to develop pancreatic cells for curing diabetes, cardiac muscle cells for curing heart disease, brain cells for curing Alzheimer's—or even entire new organs for transplantation. "There's not an area of medicine that this technology will not potentially impact," says Nobel laureate Harold Varmus.

Opponents of therapeutic cloning know all this, but are unmoved. This is because their fundamental objection is not that therapeutic cloning is antilife, but that it entails "playing God"—i.e., remaking nature to serve human purposes. "[Human cloning] would be taking a major step into making man himself simply another one of the man-made things," says Leon Kass, chairman of the President's Council on Bioethics.

"Human nature becomes merely the last part of nature to succumb to the technological project, which turns all of nature into raw material at human disposal." Columnist Armstrong Williams condemns all cloning as "human egotism, or the desire to exert our will over every aspect of our surroundings," and cautions: "We're not God."

The one truth in the anticloning position is that cloning does represent "the desire to exert our will over every aspect of our surroundings." But such a desire is not immoral—it is a mark of virtue. Using technology to alter nature is a requirement of human life. It is what brought man from the cave to civilization. Where would we be without the men who "exerted their will" over their surroundings and constructed the first hut, cottage, and skyscraper?

Every advance in human history is part of "the technological project," and has made man's life longer, healthier, and happier. These advances are produced by those who hold the premise that suffering and disease are a curse, not to be humbly accepted as "God's will," but to be fought proudly with all the power of man's rational mind.

The same virtue applies to reproductive cloning—which, despite the ridiculous, horror-movie scenarios conjured up by its opponents, would simply result in time-separated twins just as human as anyone else.

Reproductive Cloning is Ethical

Once it becomes safe, reproductive cloning will have legitimate uses for infertile couples and for preventing the transmission of genetic diseases. Even more important, it is significant as an early form of a tremendous value: *genetic engineering*, which most anticloners object to because as such it entails "playing God" with the genetic makeup of one's child. At stake with reproductive cloning is not only whether you can conceive a child who shares your genetic makeup, but whether you have the right to improve the genetic makeup of your children: to prevent them from getting genetic diseases, to prolong their lifespan or to improve their physical appearance. You should have such rights just as you have the right to vaccinate your children or to fit them with braces.

The mentalities that denounce cloning and "playing God" have consistently opposed technological progress, especially in medicine.

They objected to anesthesia, smallpox inoculations, contraception, heart transplants, in vitro fertilization—on the grounds that these innovations were "unnatural" and contrary to God's will. To let them cripple biotechnological progress by banning cloning would be a moral abomination.

CHAPTER 4

Eugenics and Genetic Engineering

Chapter Preface

No other application of technology has stimulated as much concern and debate as the potential to genetically engineer children by manipulating the human genome. The main focus of concern is genetic enhancement, which is the manipulation of the basic genetic material of a baby to improve or optimize its abilities or attributes. Although genetic enhancement of humans is not yet possible, the technology is envisioned as a way to make children smarter, more attractive, or better at athletic or artistic pursuits.

Long before technology even approached the ability to genetically engineer humans, science-fiction literature provided vivid depictions of a reality filled with genetically altered babies. One of the most lasting contributions came from Aldous Huxley's *Brave New World*. Written in 1932, Huxley's novel imagined a world in which babies are created in factories and altered genetically to fit a specific job or role in society. As one of the novel's characters describes to individuals on a tour of the Central London Hatchery and Conditioning Centre: "'We also predestine and condition. We decant our babies as socialized human beings, as Alphas or Epsilons, as future sewage workers or future . . .' He was going to say 'future World controllers,' but correcting himself, said 'future Directors of Hatcheries,' instead."

Literary visions of a stratified society based on enhanced traits and abilities are not without basis in reality. In the early twentieth century, various theoreticians believed that the science of eugenics could create a master race of people who had the most desirable traits. Eugenics, from the Greek words for "well born" or "good breeding," promotes the selective breeding of humans to enhance specific traits. Rather than focusing on genetic manipulation, the idea of eugenics is based upon the processes used at farms to mate specific animals together to encourage the inheritance of certain desirable features. Hoping to produce healthier and more intelligent citizens, scientists and politicians in the United States and Europe awarded "genetically fit" families while initiating programs to sterilize those who were considered feebleminded or otherwise undesirable. After Nazi Germany strove to form a "racially pure" society through killing and forced sterilization, eugenics took on more sinister implications.

Today, some people fear that genetic enhancement will lead in the same direction as the Nazi eugenics project. Many in the field of bioethics debate whether there is a difference between the two. The viewpoints in the following chapter examine that question as well as other controversies surrounding selective breeding, eugenics, and modern genetic engineering.

Eugenics Would Improve the Human Race

Francis Galton

In the following selection, nineteenth-century English anthro-pologist Francis Galton argues that society would be improved if humans were the best possible specimens of their species. He asserts that selective breeding of humans to enhance qualities including health, energy, ability, manliness, courteous disposition, artistic talent, curiosity, ability to concentrate, and other special aptitudes suited for each profession will improve national quality through increasing the number of individuals with these preferred traits. Galton calls this idea "eugenics" from the Greek words for "well born" or "good breeding." Galton claims that these different physical and mental qualities, including membership in the more "civilized" races, should be emphasized in the selection of the best individuals to produce children. According to Galton the policy of eugenics should begin with the education of the people so that they will understand the purpose and benefits of selective breeding. Once the population understands the goals of eugenics, he states, then a systematic process can begin to track beneficial characteristics through families and suggest selective matings that would increase the number of desirable traits.

Eugenics is the science which deals with all influences that improve the inborn qualities of a race; also with those that develop them to the utmost advantage. The improvement of the inborn qualities, or stock, of some one human population, will alone be discussed here.

What is meant by improvement? What by the syllable *Eu* in eugenics, whose English equivalent is *good*? There is considerable difference between goodness in the several qualities and in that of the character as a whole. The character depends

Francis Galton, *Essays in Eugenics*. London, UK: Eugenics Society, 1909.

largely on the *proportion* between qualities whose balance may be much influenced by education. We must therefore leave morals as far as possible out of the discussion, not entangling ourselves with the almost hopeless difficulties they raise as to whether a character as a whole is good or bad. Moreover, the goodness or badness of character is not absolute, but relative to the current form of civilization. A fable will best explain what is meant. Let the scene be the [London] Zoological Gardens in the quiet hours of the night, and suppose that, as in old fables, the animals are able to converse, and that some very wise creature who had easy access to all the cages, say a philosophic sparrow or rat, was engaged in collecting the opinions of all sorts of animals with a view of elaborating a system of absolute morality. It is needless to enlarge on the contrariety of ideals between the beasts that prey and those they prey upon, between those of the animals that have to work hard for their food and the sedentary parasites that cling to their bodies and suck their blood, and so forth. A large number of suffrages in favour of maternal affection would be obtained, but most species of fish would repudiate it, while among the voices of birds would be heard the musical protest of the cuckoo. Though no agreement could be reached as to absolute morality, the essentials of eugenics may be easily defined. All creatures would agree that it was better to be healthy than sick, vigorous than weak, well-fitted than ill-fitted for their part in life. In short that it was better to be good rather than bad specimens of their kind, whatever that kind might be. So with men. There are a vast number of conflicting ideals of alternative characters, of incompatible civilizations; but all are wanted to give fullness and interest to life. Society would be very dull if every man resembled the highly estimable [Roman Emperor and Philosopher-King] Marcus Aurelius or Adam Bede [the stalwart, forthright carpenter character created by George Eliot]. The aim of Eugenics is to represent each class or sect by its best specimens; that done, to leave them to work out their common civilization in their own way.

Important Human Qualities

A considerable list of qualities can be easily compiled that nearly every one except "cranks" would take into account when picking out the best specimens of his class. It would include health, energy, ability, manliness and courteous disposition. Recollect that the natural differences between dogs are highly marked in all these respects, and that men are quite as variable by nature as other animals in their respective species. Special aptitudes would be assessed highly by those who possessed them, as the artistic faculties by artists, fearlessness of inquiry and veracity by scientists, religious absorption by mystics, and so on. There would be self-sacrificers, self-tormentors and other exceptional idealists, but the representatives of these would be better members of a community than the body of their electors. They would have more of those qualities that are needed in a State, more vigour, more ability, and more consistency of purpose. The community might be trusted to refuse representatives of criminals, and of others whom it rates as undesirable.

Let us for a moment suppose that the practice of Eugenics should hereafter raise the average quality of our nation to that of its better moiety [half] at the present day and consider the gain. The general tone of domestic, social and political life would be higher. The race as a whole would be less foolish, less frivolous, less excitable and politically more provident than now. Its demagogues who "played to the gallery" would play to a more sensible gallery than at present. We should be better fitted to fulfil our vast imperial opportunities. Lastly, men of an order of ability which is now very rare, would become more frequent, because the level out of which they rose would itself have risen.

The Aim of Eugenics

The aim of Eugenics is to bring as many influences as can be reasonably employed, to cause the useful classes in the community to contribute *more* than their proportion to the next generation.

The course of procedure that lies within the functions of a learned and active Society such as the Sociological may become, would be somewhat as follows:—

1. Dissemination of a knowledge of the laws of heredity so far as they are surely known, and promotion of their farther study. Few seem to be aware how greatly the knowledge of what may be termed the *actuarial* side of heredity has advanced in recent years. The *average* closeness of kinship in each degree now admits of exact definition and of being treated mathematically, like birth and death-rates, and the other topics with which actuaries are concerned.

2. Historical inquiry into the rates with which the various classes of society (classified according to civic usefulness) have contributed to the population at various times, in ancient and modern nations. There is strong reason for believing that national rise and decline is closely connected with this influence. It seems to be the tendency of high civilisation to check fertility in the upper classes, through numerous causes, some of which are well known, others are inferred, and others again are wholly obscure. The latter class are apparently analogous to those which bar the fertility of most species of wild animals in zoological gardens. Out of the hundreds and thousands of species that have been tamed, very few indeed are fertile when their liberty is restricted and their struggles for livelihood are abolished; those which are so and are otherwise useful to man becoming domesticated. There is perhaps some connection between this obscure action and the disappearance of most savage races when brought into contact with high civilization, though there are other and well-known concomitant causes. But while most barbarous races disappear, some, like the negro, do not. It may therefore be expected that types of our race will be found to exist which can be highly civilised

without losing fertility; nay, they may become more fertile under artificial conditions, as is the case with many domestic animals.

3. Systematic collection of facts showing the circumstances under which large and thriving families have most frequently originated; in other words, the *conditions* of Eugenics. The names of the thriving families in England have yet to be learnt, and the conditions under which they have arisen. We cannot hope to make much advance in the science of Eugenics without a careful study of facts that are now accessible with difficulty, if at all. The definition of a thriving family, such as will pass muster for the moment at least is one in which the children have gained distinctly superior positions to those who were their class-mates in early life. Families may be considered "large" that contain not less than three adult male children. It would be no great burden to a Society including many members who had Eugenics at heart, to initiate and to preserve a large collection of such records for the use of statistical students. The committee charged with the task would have to consider very carefully the form of their circular and the persons entrusted to distribute it. The circular should be simple, and as brief as possible, consistent with asking all questions that are likely to be answered truly, and which would be important to the inquiry. They should ask, at least in the first instance, only for as much information as could be easily, and would be readily, supplied by any member of the family appealed to. The point to be ascertained is the *status* of the two parents at the time of their marriage, whence its more or less eugenic character might have been predicted, if the larger knowledge that we now hope to obtain had then existed. Some account would, of course, be wanted of their race, profession, and residence; also of their own respective parentages, and of their brothers and sisters. Finally, the reasons would be required why the children deserved to be entitled a "thriving" family, to distinguish worthy from unworthy success. This

manuscript collection might hereafter develop into a "golden book" of thriving families. The Chinese, whose customs have often much sound sense, make their honours retrospective. We might learn from them to show that respect to the parents of note-worthy children, which the contributors of such valuable assets to the national wealth richly deserve. The act of systematically collecting records of thriving families would have the further advantage of familiarising the public with the fact that Eugenics had at length become a subject of serious scientific study by an energetic Society.

4. Influences affecting Marriage. The remarks of Lord [Francis] Bacon [the English philosopher, statesman, and essayist] in his essay on Death may appropriately be quoted here. He says with the view of minimising its terrors:

> "There is no passion in the mind of men so weak but it mates and masters the fear of death.—Revenge triumphs over death; love slights it; honour aspireth to it; grief flyeth to it; fear pre-occupateth it."

Exactly the same kind of considerations apply to marriage. The passion of love seems so overpowering that it may be thought folly to try to direct its course. But plain facts do not confirm this view. Social influences of all kinds have immense power in the end, and they are very various. If unsuitable marriages from the Eugenic point of view were banned socially, or even regarded with the unreasonable disfavour which some attach to cousin-marriages, very few would be made. The multitude of marriage restrictions that have proved prohibitive among uncivilized people would require a volume to describe.

5. Persistence in setting forth the national importance of Eugenics. There are three stages to be passed through. *Firstly* it must be made familiar as an academic question, until its exact importance has been understood and accepted as a fact; *Secondly* it must be recognised as a subject whose practical development deserves serious consideration; and *Thirdly* it must be

introduced into the national conscience, like a new religion. It has, indeed, strong claims to become an orthodox religious tenet of the future, for Eugenics co-operates with the workings of Nature by securing that humanity shall be represented by the fittest races. What Nature does blindly, slowly, and ruthlessly, man may do providently, quickly, and kindly. As it lies within his power, so it becomes his duty to work in that direction; just as it is his duty to succour neighbours who suffer misfortune. The improvement of our stock seems to me one of the highest objects that we can reasonably attempt. We are ignorant of the ultimate destinies of humanity, but feel perfectly sure that it is as noble a work to raise its level in the sense already explained, as it would be disgraceful to abase it. I see no impossibility in Eugenics becoming a religious dogma among mankind, but its details must first be worked out sedulously in the study. Over-zeal leading to hasty action would do harm, by holding out expectations of a near golden age, which will certainly be falsified and cause the science to be discredited. The first and main point is to secure the general intellectual acceptance of Eugenics as a hopeful and most important study. Then let its principles work into the heart of the nation, who will gradually give practical effect to them in ways that we may not wholly foresee.

Setting Ethical Standards for Medical Research Involving Humans

Ralph Slovenko

In the following selection, Ralph Slovenko discusses the development of bioethical standards for the protection of human subjects in the twentieth century. He describes unethical experiments, like those carried out by Tuskegee syphilis researchers in the United States and the Nazi physicians in Germany, that prompted the adoption of standards of ethical practice. Slovenko pays special attention to the establishment of the universal policy requiring informed consent of test subjects and the standard practice by which research trials are overseen by institutional review boards.

Ralph Slovenko is a Professor of Law and Psychiatry at Wayne State University Law School in Detroit, Michigan. He is editor of the American Series in Behavioral Science and Law *and a regular commentator in the* Journal of Psychiatry and Law.

Standards for experimental treatment or for research involving human subjects has been a major development of the 20th century. They came about in response to horrendous experiments carried out by Nazi Germany and also in the United States and elsewhere. After World War II, the United States and its allies were involved in a succession of criminal trials that have become known as the Nuremberg Trials. Perhaps the best known Nuremberg trial involved the military officers of the Third Reich. The "Doctors' Trial," also known as the "Medical Case," was tried at the Palace of Justice in postwar Nuremberg under U.S. military auspices. Those appointed by President Truman to hear the "Medical Case" were all Ameri-

Ralph Slovenko, "The Evolution of Standards for Experimental Treatment or Research," *Journal of Psychiatry & Law*, vol. 33, Spring 2005, pp. 129–39, 142–43, 155–56. Copyright © 2005 by Federal Legal Publications, Inc. Reproduced by permission.

can judges and lawyers; the case was prosecuted by then Supreme Court Justice Robert Jackson and by Telford Taylor, a military lawyer.

The Nuremberg tribunal was asked to determine the culpability of 23 German physicians under "the principles of the law of nations as they result from the usages established among civilized peoples, from the laws of humanity, and from the dictates of public conscience." The trial was a murder trial (murder was identified by the tribunal as a crime against humanity). For weeks the prosecution cited acts such as the use of Jewish prisoners in medical experiments to determine the limits of high-altitude flying by locking them in pressure chambers, slowly rupturing their lungs and skulls. Prisoners were submerged in icy water until they died so as to determine how long downed German pilots could last in the ocean. To develop a blood-clotting chemical, the physicians shot and dismembered live prisoners to simulate battlefield conditions.

Throughout the trial, the question was presented of what were or should be the universal standards for justifying human experimentation. The alleged lack of a universally accepted principle for carrying out human experimentation was the central issue pressed by the defendant physicians. (The Japanese carried out deadly medical experiments on prisoners in Manchuria long before the Nazi doctors, but they were never tried.) A few of the ethical arguments presented by the defendants during the trial at Nuremberg as justification for their participation in the experimentation programs were:

> (1) Only people who were doomed to die were used in the experiments. (2) Research is necessary in times of national emergency. Military and civilian survival may depend on the scientific and medical knowledge derived from human experimentation. Extreme circumstances demand extreme action. (3) There were no universal standards of research ethics. (4) The state determined the necessity for the human experimentation. The physicians were merely following or-

ders. (5) Sometimes it is necessary to tolerate a lesser evil, the killing of some, to achieve a greater good, the saving of many. (6) The prisoners' consent to participation in human experimentation was tacit. Since there were no statements that the subjects did not consent, it should be assumed that valid consent existed. (7) Participation in research offered expiation to the subjects for their crimes (that is, polluting German society). (8) The Hippocratic Oath was not betrayed, as Jews posed a public health problem, a "disease" that contaminated the body politic.

Eugenics in the United States and Nazi Germany

Actually Nazi Germany learned much about eugenics from the United States. At the turn of the 20th century, melting-pot America provided fertile soil for eugenics. (In 1883 Sir Francis Galton, a cousin of Charles Darwin, coined the term "eugenics," which derives from the Greek word for "well-born.") The "science" of eugenics would improve the human stock by giving the more suitable races or strains of blood a better chance of prevailing speedily over the less suitable than they otherwise would have. The U.S. eugenics movement was funded by the industrial titans of the country—Andrew Carnegie, John D. Rockefeller, Jr., and Mary Harriman, widow of the railroad magnate Edward Harriman—and was championed by graduates of Harvard, Yale, and other Ivy League universities. . . .

The United States at the time segregated blacks, prohibited miscegenation, outlawed homosexual behavior, carried out risky experiments on captive populations, and sterilized thousands of mentally retarded individuals, not to mention the earlier decimation of the Indian population. In 1927 the U.S. Supreme Court ruled by an 8-1 majority that eugenic sterilization was constitutional. . . .

Editorials in *The New York Times* and leading medical journals like *The New England Journal of Medicine* wrote positively about eugenic sterilization. By 1945 some 45,127 people in the United States had been sterilized, 21,311 of them patients in mental hospitals.

Prior to World War I, eugenics was not nearly as popular in Germany as it was in the United States; sterilization at that time was illegal in Germany. But after [Adolf] Hitler came to power in 1933, Germany passed a comprehensive sterilization bill. The leaders in the German sterilization movement stated repeatedly that their legislation was formulated only after studying experiments in the United States. Over the next six years, Germany sterilized 375,000 of its citizens. The fervor with which Germany was carrying out sterilization prompted some American eugenicists to fret that Hitler was now "beating us at our own game."

In carrying out their experiments, the Nazi doctors believed there was a moral basis for doing what they did. They gloried in their endeavors. The eugenic philosophy of the time valued the lives of some more than others. The Jews and others killed or maimed in the experiments were considered inferior beings, and the knowledge to be gained might save the lives of superior Germans. Anyhow, experimentation or not, the Jews and others would be put to death. The "unfit" were doomed to *ausmerze* (extinction) that would be carried out in a way that would give barbarism and sadism a new meaning. . . .

The Nuremberg Code

In 1947 the American judges [at the Nuremberg Trials] found 15 of the 23 doctors guilty and sentenced seven to death by hanging. Two American physicians who testified for the prosecution, physiologist Andrew Ivy and neuropsychiatrist Leo Alexander, contributed to the writing of the ten-point Nuremberg Code for ethical human experimentation. At the heart of the code—its first point—was the principle that the interests of science should never take precedence over the rights of the human subject. Research subjects were not to be taken as means to a scientific end, and they needed to always give informed consent. That principle in the code was put in absolute terms: "The voluntary consent of the human subject is *absolutely* essential. This means [the capacity] to exercise free power of choice without the intervention of any element of force, fraud, deceit, duress, overreaching, or other ulterior form of constraint or coercion" (emphasis added). To be sure, a morality code addressed to the medical profession such as the Nuremberg Code is not needed in order to condemn such practices as those of the Nazi doctors. They committed crimes.

Informed Consent

The doctrine of "informed consent" was not an invention of American law or ethics. A legal requirement for the informed consent of the subject of human experimentation was earlier made in a ministerial directive issued in Berlin in 1900. . . .

In the United States the concept of informed consent in experimentation originated in the clinical care setting. The first U.S. case to use the term "informed consent" was in 1957 in *Salvo v. Leland Stanford, Jr. University Board of Trustees*. It ruled that patients must not only freely consent but also must be fully informed about treatment options. The legal concept was essentially developed to provide a cause of action in cases of poor outcome when negligence in treatment could not be established, and it later also became a medical ethic. . . .

Unethical Research in the United States

The events described at the Nuremberg Trials have not been perceived by researchers or commentators to be directly relevant to the American scene. As a consequence the United States, in conducting the "Doctors' Trial," presented itself as the country that would insist that science be carried out in a moral manner. But the reality was that gross misuse of humans in research occurred in the United States not only before but also after the formulation of the Nuremberg Code.

Journalist Robert Whitaker has noted: "[T]he ink on the Nuremberg Code was barely dry when Paul Hoch, director of research at the New York State Psychiatric Institute, began giving LSD and mescaline to schizophrenics in order to investigate the 'chemistry' of psychosis." . . .

Ultimately, research scandals in the United States provided the political impetus to institute formal protections for research subjects, to complete the work begun with the Nuremberg Code. In 1966 Henry K. Beecher, a professor of research in anesthesia at Harvard Medical School, published a widely discussed article identifying 22 examples of objectionable research. Although the article did not lead to immediate change, it did more than the Nuremberg Code to sensitize the medical community to the protection of subjects. Only six pages long, it was devastating in its indictment of research ethics. . . .

It was a long-running Tuskegee study that finally moved the United States toward a systematic formal regulation of research standards. In 1932 the government had initiated an observational study of syphilis in African-American men that did not end until a journalist brought it to national attention in 1972. The aim of the study was to learn whether syphilis had a different pathological course in black men than in white men. For decades infected subjects were not treated, even though an effective therapy had become widely available. In fact, the researchers actively conspired with physicians in the area to prevent these subjects from obtaining treatment. The repercussions remain to this day as African-Americans, mindful of the study, are wary of experimentation.

Human Subject Protection Strengthened

In 1974 Congress approved the National Research Act and established an advisory body, the National Commission for the Protection of Human Subjects of Biomedical and Behavioral Research. It also required that all research funded by the Department of Health, Education, and Welfare receive prior review and approval from local review committees. The National Research Act established the system of Institutional Review Boards (IRBs), local committees that determine whether certain standards of subject protection are met before research may commence. . . .

The work of the National Commission also led to the influential 1978 Belmont Report, which identified three main concepts by which to evaluate the ethics of research: (1) respect for persons, (2) beneficence, and (3) justice. Respect for persons stresses the importance of recognizing persons as their own decision makers and protecting those who are unable to make decisions for themselves (researchers must offer potential subjects adequate information about the project, ensure that subjects comprehend the information, and ensure the voluntary nature of participation). The concept of beneficence asserts the importance of protecting the welfare of subjects (it requires researchers to offer a meaningful balance of risks and benefits). And justice requires that no particular group is favored in access to and distribution of research benefits. The IRBs have the responsibility of implementing these concepts as embodied in federal regulations. The nature and scope of oversight remain a matter of continuing debate. . . .

Research and Physicians

The Belmont Report, which served as the foundation for the federal regulations for the protection of human subjects, outlines the boundaries between research and clinical practice. Delineating those boundaries was important because physicians could otherwise "cloak" research under standard-of-care practices. The Belmont Report states that if any portion of a patient's therapy is experimental, the treatment or strategy must be reviewed for the protection of human subjects. . . .

Of combining research and practice, Beecher warned that the relationship between physician-investigator and patient-subject is one that can easily be manipulated. He pointed out:

"If suitably approached, patients will accede, on the basis of trust, to about any request their physicians may make." . . .

The Need for Human Research

There are limits, however, to what people may consent to. Not all apparent exercises of autonomy are tolerated. Consent, for example, is no defense to a charge of murder, or to render the infliction of other serious injuries lawful. However, for medical research, human beings may be used, within limits, as guinea pigs. Public policy accepts the value of research. Without tests on human subjects, progress in medicine would be handicapped or stymied. Much of the medical progress that has benefited humanity would have been impossible without human subject research. This progress was accomplished primarily through clinical drug or device trials, psychological evaluations, studies of environmental hazards, and many other avenues. . . .

The shadow of the Nazi experiments, though the ideology of that day has waned, continues to hover over experimentation with prisoners. People in captivity, as a matter of law, may not consent to experimentation for fear that they may be enticed by special treatment or early release, though in reality they may be more competent and informed than those suffering various kinds of mental incapacity for whom voluntary consent is no longer "absolutely" essential. Today there are criminal and tort laws to ensure (except in the military) that those doing research with human beings are using sound scientific designs, have the consent, however imperfect, of their subjects, have no conflict of interest in undertaking or interpreting their findings, and can obtain relevant information about what other researchers are doing in a timely manner. IRBs, whatever their shortcomings, cause researchers to pause and consider the ethics of their experiment, or else to go to other countries to carry out their research.

Parents Have a Duty to Make Better Children through Genetic Enhancement

Julian Savulescu

The implications of enhancing or genetically engineering children before birth have stimulated extensive international ethical debate. In the following selection, Julian Savulescu, professor and chair in Practical Ethics at the University of Oxford, argues that parents have the same moral obligation to enhance certain traits in their children through genetic technology before birth as they have to treat and prevent disease in their children after birth. He also maintains that genetic enhancement is no different than the myriad ways in which parents strive to improve their children's lives. In fact, he claims, to fail to enhance children may be to deprive them of the opportunities afforded to enhanced peers.

The genophobe claims that it is our environment, or culture, that defines us, not genetics. But a quiet walk in the park demonstrates the power of that great genetic experiment: dog breeding. It is obvious that different breeds of dogs differ in temperament, intelligence, physical ability and appearance. No matter what the turf, doberman will tear a corgi to pieces. Of course, you can debilitate a doberman through neglect and abuse. And you can make him prettier with a bow. But you will never turn a chihuahua into a doberman through grooming, training and affection. Dog breeds are all genetic—for over ten thousand years we have bred some 300–400 breeds of dog from early canids and wolves. . . . These characteristics have been developed by a crude form of genetic selection—selective mating or breeding. . . .

Julian Savulescu, "New Breeds of Humans: The Moral Obligation to Enhance," *Reproductive BioMedicine Online*, vol. 10, December 9, 2005, pp. 36–39. www.rbmonline.com.

Selective mating has been occurring in humans ever since time began. Facial asymmetry can reflect genetic disorder. Smell can tell us whether our mate will produce the child with the best resistance to disease. We compete for partners in elaborate mating games and rituals of display which sort the best matches from the worst. As products of evolution, we select our mates, both rationally and instinctively, on the basis of their genetic fitness—their ability to survive and reproduce. Our goal is the success of our offspring.

With the tools of genetics, we can select offspring in a more reliable way. The power of genetics is growing. Embryos can now be tested not only for the presence of genetic disorder (including some forms of bowel and breast cancer), but also for less serious genetic abnormalities, such as dental abnormalities. Sex can be tested for too. Adult athletes have been genetically tested for the presence of the angiotensin converting enzyme (ACE) gene to identify potential Olympic athletes. Research is going on in the field of behavioural genetics to understand the genetic basis of aggression and criminal behaviour, alcoholism, anxiety, antisocial personality disorder, maternal behaviour, homosexuality and neuroticism.

While at present there are no genetic tests for these complex behaviours, if the results of recent animal studies into hard work and monogamy apply to humans, it may be possible in the future to genetically change how we are predisposed to behave. This raises a new question.

Should We Decide What Breed of Humans to Create?

Some people in society believe that children are a gift, of God or of Nature, and that we should not interfere in human nature. Must people implicitly reject this view—we screen embryos and fetuses for diseases, even mild correctable diseases. We interfere in Nature or God's will when we vaccinate, provide pain relief to women in labour (despite objections of some earlier Christians that these practices thwarted God's will) and treat cancer. It is nevertheless true that we believe it is a parent's duty to unconditionally love and accept a child, even if that child is involved in an accident and is left horribly disabled.

The reason that genetic selection is not ingratitude and intolerance for the gift of life is because the life in question is not yet the life of a child. Destruction of early human embryos and fetuses is not infanticide. People in Western societies have voted with their feet about the moral status of early human life. One hundred thousand abortions per year in the UK speak to the value of early human life. If we were really serious that embryos were people, we would force couples undergoing IVF to donate spare embryos to other infertile couples, just as we force couples who do not or cannot care for their children to have them adopted by other couples. But of course, most people do not really believe embryos are children.

More importantly, no one would object to the treatment of disability in a child, if it were possible. Why, then, not treat the embryo with genetic therapy if that intervention is safe? Even though not a child, it might later be a child. And better that child without disability than with disability. This is no more thwarting God's will than giving antibiotics is.

The Moral Obligation to Enhance Our Children

Many people would accept my claim that there is a moral imperative to treat and prevent disease. A parent who knowingly failed to protect his or her child from contracting HIV through a simple and safe intervention would be considered guilty of a moral crime. Many people will accept genetic selection to avoid disease. Many may even come to accept germline gene therapy, if it is safe, under the moral imperative to treat disease and promote health. I believe the same moral obligation exists to enhance our children's lives and opportunities.

What Matters Is Well-Being

It is the goodness of health that drives a moral obligation to treat or prevent disease. Being healthy enables us to lead a good life. But health is not intrinsically valuable. It is instrumentally valuable—valuable as a resource that allows us to do what really matters, that is, lead a good life. . .

But if it is well-being not health that is intrinsically valuable we can see why human enhancement can become a moral obligation. Many of our biological and psychological characteristics profoundly affect how well our lives go. In the 1960s, Walter Mischel conducted impulse control experiments where four-year-old children were left in a room with one marshmallow, after being told that if they did not eat the marshmallow, they could later have two. Some children would eat it as soon as the researcher left, others would use a variety of strategies to help control their behaviour and ignore the temptation of the single marshmallow. A decade later, they reinterviewed the children and found that those who were better at delaying gratification had more friends, better academic performance and more motivation to succeed. Whether the child had grabbed for the marshmallow had a much stronger bearing on their standardized attainment test (SAT) scores than did their IQ. . . .

Intelligence, of many kinds: memory, temperament, patience, empathy, a sense of humour, optimism and just having a sunny temperament can profoundly affect our lives. All of these characteristics will have some biological and psychological basis capable of manipulation with technology.

If we have an obligation to treat and prevent disease, we have an obligation to try to manipulate these characteristics to give an individual the best opportunity of the best life.

Evolution was previously about the selection of genes according to environment which conferred the greatest chance of survival and reproduction. Evolution would select a tribe which was highly fertile but suffered great pain the whole of their lives over another tribe which was less fertile but suffered less pain. Medicine has changed evolution—we can now select individuals who experience less pain and disease. The next stage of human evolution may be rational evolution, where we select children who not only have the greatest chance of surviving, reproducing and being free of disease, but who also have the greatest opportunities to have the best lives. Evolution was indifferent to how well our lives went. We are not. We want to retire, play golf, read and watch our grandchildren have children.

Enhancement is a misnomer. It suggests luxury. But enhancement is no luxury. In so far as it promotes well-being, it is the very essence of what is necessary for a good human life.

Why Enhancement Is the Right Course

Once technology affords us with the power to enhance our and our children's lives, to fail to do so will be to be responsible for the consequences. To fail to treat our children's disease is to harm them. To fail to prevent them getting depression is to harm them. To fail to improve their physical, musical, psychological and other capacities is to harm them, just as it would be to harm them if we gave them a toxic substance that stunted or reduced these capacities.

There are other arguments for enhancement. It may benefit parents and society. Consistency also requires it. We laud parents who sacrifice themselves to provide the best educational opportunities for their children, or who attempt to produce well-behaved good children. But the environment only acts to affect our biology. If we accept environmental manipulations, by force of consistency we must accept genetic or other biological manipulations that are safe and have the same effects. And biological enhancements may ultimately provide much greater increases in our childrens' opportunities than the school we send them to. . . .

One of the major objections to enhancement is that it is against human nature. Common alternative phrasings are that enhancement is tampering with our nature, that it is hubris, or an affront to human dignity. I believe that what separates us from other animals is our nationality, our capacity to make normative judgements and act on the basis of reasons. When we make decisions to improve lives by biological and other manipulations, we express our rationality and express what is fundamentally important about our nature. And if those manipulations improve our capacity to make rational and normative judgements, they further improve what is fundamentally human. Far from being against the human spirit, such improvements express the human spirit. . . .

In my opinion, many enhancements will have both positional and non-positional qualities. Intelligence is good not just because it allows an individual to be more competitive for complex jobs, but because it allows an individual to process information more rapidly in her own life, and to develop greater understanding of herself and others. These non-positional effects should not be ignored.

Nonetheless, if there are significant social consequences of enhancement, this is of course a valid objection. But it is not particular to enhancement—there is an old question about how far individuals in society can pursue their own self-interest at cost to others. It applies to education, health care, and virtually all areas of life. It requires a theory of justice to resolve.

Not all enhancements will be ethical. The critical issue is that the intervention is expected to bring about more benefits than harms to the individual. It must be safe and there must be a reasonable expectation of improvement. . . .

Enhancement Is Not Eugenics

Many will argue that such a proposal is eugenic. Eugenics was the movement early last century which aimed to use selective breeding to prevent degeneration of the gene pool by weeding out criminals, those with mental illness and the poor, on the false belief that these conditions were simple genetic disorders. The eugenics movement had its inglorious peak when the Nazis moved beyond sterilization to extermination of the genetically unfit.

What was objectionable about the eugenics movement, besides its shoddy scientific basis, was that it involved the imposition of a state vision for a healthy population and aimed to achieve this through coercion. The eugenics movement was not aimed at what was good for individuals, but rather at what benefited society. Modern eugenics in the form of testing for disorders, such as Down's syndrome, occurs very commonly but is considered acceptable because it is voluntary, gives couples a choice over what kind of child to have and enables them to have a child with the greatest opportunity for a good life.

The critical question to ask in considering whether to alter some gene related to complex behaviour is: would the change be better for the individual? Is it better for the individual to have a tendency to be lazy or hardworking: monogamous or polygamous? These questions are difficult to answer.

There will be cases where some intervention is plausibly in a person's interests: empathy with other people, capacity to understand oneself and the world around, memory. One quality is especially associated with socio-economic success and staying out of prison: impulse control. If it were possible to correct poor impulse control, we should correct it. Whether we should remove impulsiveness altogether is another question.

Our future is in our hands now, whether we like it or not. But by not allowing enhancement and control over the genetic nature of our offspring, we consign a person to the natural lottery, and now, by having the power to do otherwise, to fail to do otherwise is to be responsible for the results of the natural lottery. We must make a choice: the natural lottery or rational choice. Where an enhancement is plausibly good for an individual, we should let that individual decide. And in the case of the next generation, we should let parents decide. To fail to allow them to make these choices is to consign the next generation to the ball and chain of our squeamishness and irrationality. . . .

To most of us, the choice is obvious. To be human is to be better. Or, at least, to strive to be better.

Prenatal Genetic Screening Is a New Form of Eugenics

C. Ben Mitchell

The ability of physicians in the twenty-first century to test babies for genetic diseases before birth has allowed parents to know if their child is affected by certain genetic disorders early in their gestation. In the following selection, bioethics professor C. Ben Mitchell asserts that genetic testing before birth is an unacceptable return to the unethical eugenic principles of human selection. Mitchell argues that in eliminating embryos affected by genetic conditions, technology could be preventing the birth of an individual who would have been a great asset to society. Mitchell feels that testing before birth will lead to a change in society's mindset so that individuals who are less than perfect will not be accepted. He urges rejection of this eugenic thinking.

Preimplantation genetic screening is the latest assault against a truly human future. According to a report in the 27 February [2005] *Journal of the American Medical Association*, a 30-year-old woman has chosen to use the technique because she carries the rare gene for early onset Alzheimer's disease. This particular variety of Alzheimer's reportedly affects adults by the time they are 40 years of age.

The unidentified woman had a baby girl who is allegedly free from the Alzheimer's gene because she was selected from a number of embryos, some of whom presumably had the gene and were therefore destroyed.

Prenatal Screening

Prenatal genetic screening may be performed either before implantation or in utero [within the womb]. In preimplantation

C. Ben Mitchell, "Hurtling Toward Eugenics . . . Again," *Ethics & Medicine*, vol. 18, Summer 2002, pp. 3–5. Reproduced by permission of the author.

screening, embryos are tested for certain genetic conditions and either implanted or destroyed depending on the wishes of the prospective parents. In post-implantation screening, unborn children are tested in the womb to see if they are carrying deleterious genes and either carried to term or aborted.

Previously, almost all prenatal genetic screening was used in connection with abortion decisions. Since there are so few genetic therapies, prospective parents are faced either with the knowledge that their child will carry a disease gene when he or she is born or may decide to terminate the pregnancy through abortion. Some parents who would not choose embryo selection or abortion may refuse prenatal genetic testing, since they intend to bring a child to term regardless of genetic condition. Others may find the information important as they prepare for a child who may have disabilities.

In this case, embryos were created using in vitro fertilization techniques, and the embryos were genetically screened. "Acceptable" embryos were implanted and "undesirable" embryos were destroyed or may have been used in research. But who decides what is a disease gene and what is merely a different genetic condition? Who decides who is a "desirable" or "undesirable" embryo?

Rutgers University sociologist Marque-Louisa Miringoff has observed:

> In the pursuit of good health, we have begun to tread a fine line in "human selection." We often choose to rule out certain diseases or, more accurately, certain human beings with those diseases. In some cases, as with Tay-Sachs disease, an as of now invariably fatal illness in early childhood, such a decision may be motivated by compassion. From many viewpoints, there is little quality of life in any sense traditionally understood, and great anguish and tragedy.

> Other diseases, however, challenge our logic more severely; our sense of balance between cost and benefit is not clear. Huntington's chorea is a case in point. Would a Woodie

Guthrie be born today? Would his parents, as carriers of the disease, bear a child with the known risk? Could we now or soon screen him out prenatally? If the pace of genetic intervention continues, such an individual would not be born. Yet, I for one, am glad that he lived, although I mourn the anguish of his later life. One wonders, too, whether some perception of his coming illness contributed to the extraordinary creativity of his life.

Clearly, it is a just and meaningful desire to prevent fatal and debilitating diseases. Yet in pursuing this goal, we pay unobserved costs. In eliminating individuals with unwanted diseases, we also create a mind-set that justifies the process of human selection. We thus move into the questionable arena of human worth, and to some degree eugenic thought. We forgo the idea of therapeutic change (i.e., dietary change or other forms of treatment) and opt instead for elimination. Individuals are seen as flawed. It is easier and more desirable to prevent their existence than to work for their survival.

Who knows who the other "Alzheimer's children" might have grown up to be? Might they have been the next Woody Guthrie, Beethoven, Mozart, or Bach? Might they have been the brilliant scientists who discovered the cure for their own disease? We will never know because they were selected out as an "undesirable."

The New Eugenics

"Eugenics" is a compound word from two Greek words meaning "good" and "genes." The eugenics movement began at the turn of the last century in England and the United States. Under the leadership of social engineers such as Francis Galton and Charles Davenport, the eugenics movement became a powerful social force.

So-called "Fitter Families" contests were held across the United States in the 1920s and 1930s. Fitter families were families with fewer incidences of physical and mental disability. Their ethnic heritage also had to remain intact. Racial intermarriage disqualified families. Thus, the fitter families were exclusively Caucasian. Mary T. Watts, co-founder of the first contest at the 1920 Kansas Free Fair, said: "While the stock judges are testing the Holsteins, Jerseys, and white-faces in the stock pavilion, we are judging the Joneses, Smiths, and Johns." Winners were given a medal inscribed with the slogan, "Yea, I Have a Goodly Heritage."

The eugenics movement tried to create "better humans through better breeding." Yet breeding was not the only way to achieve the desired goals. In order to prevent "undesirables" from reproducing, mandatory sterilization laws were enacted. The "feebleminded," "indolent," and "licentious" were sterilized either without their consent or against their wills. So-called "eugenical sterilizations" increased from around 3,000 in 1907 to over 22,000 in 1935. By the 1930s most states had mandatory sterilization laws. In one well-known case, a young mentally retarded girl named Carrie Buck was given the "choice" either to be sterilized or to be returned to her asylum. Because both her mother and grandmother had been mentally retarded, the famous jurist Oliver Wendall Holmes declared of Carrie Buck, "three generations of imbeciles is enough" and mandated that she be sterilized. . . .

With the power of genetic technology, a new eugenics has emerged. A 1993 March of Dimes poll found that 11% of parents said they would abort a fetus whose genome was predisposed to obesity. Four out of five would abort a fetus if it would grow up with a disability. Forty-three percent said they would use genetic engineering if available simply to enhance their child's appearance.

Increasingly, college age women are being solicited for their donor eggs on the basis of their desirable genetic traits. In the summer of 2000, the Minnesota Daily, the student newspaper of the University of Minnesota, ran an ad for egg donors. Preferred donors were women 5 foot six inches or taller, Caucasian, with high ACT or SAT scores, with no genetic illnesses, and extra compensation was offered to those with mathematical, musical, or athletic abilities. The ad stated that acceptable donors would be offered as much as $80,000 for their eggs.

Preimplantation genetic screening is another weapon in the eugenics arsenal. This case puts our feet more than half way down the slippery slope. Selection of our offspring has never been easier. Embryonic death has never been more acceptable in our culture. This is eugenics with a vengeance.

Our culture's emphasis on the genetically "fit" and our difficulty in embracing those who are "less fit" fuels this new eugenics mindset. We must resist the new eugenicists if we are to preserve a truly human future.

Chronology

B.C.

2250

Hammurabi's Babylonian Code addresses medical ethics issues and physician responsibility for patient outcome by mandating formal fees for treatment and specific punishments for inept physicians.

421

The Greek physician Hippocrates establishes a medical school and develops codes of physician conduct that define the ethical behavior of medical practioners.

161–138

The Roman emperor Antoninus Pius restricts the number of physicians allowed per town, but also sets up physician payment through town officials and exempts them from paying taxes and some public duties. Pius also requires certain tests of character and ability to ensure a unified degree of physician competence.

25 B.C.–A.D. 40

The ancient Roman author Aulus Cornelius Celsus emphasizes the value of learning from past medical errors so that the same mistakes will not be made in the future.

A.D.

300–476

The rise of Christianity ushers in a new set of morals and beliefs over the waning Roman medical ethics and moral theory.

1215

The Christian Church develops lengthy treatises and manuals on moral theology that include guidelines for physicians; the Church also emphasizes that experimenting on patients (especially the poor) is a sin if it puts them at risk.

1300s

Medieval physicians recover, translate, and utilize classical texts on medical ethics.

1518

Sir Thomas Linacre founds the College of Physicians in London in order to improve the member physicians' practice and morals.

1743–1773

Physicians such as John Gregory develop new moral philosophies during the Scottish Enlightenment; these concepts are integrated with ancient teachings to create a medical code that emphasizes a doctor's duty to the sympathetic and lifelong treatment of patients.

1803

English physician Thomas Percival becomes the first doctor to develop formal medical ethical codes for surgeons and physicians.

1832

Physicians found the British Medical Association; one of its objectives is to maintain the honor and respectability of the profession.

1847

The American Medical Association (AMA) adopts its first code of ethics based on Thomas Percival's writings.

1900–1947

Nazi Germany, the United States, and Japan engage in unethical human research; after the full extent of such experiments is uncovered in the mid- to late twentieth century, scientists, politicians, and physicians develop guidelines to provide universal protection for human subjects.

1932–1971

The Tuskegee Public Health Syphilis Study recruits hundreds of African American men with and without syphilis to participate in a study of the disease; the men are subjected to unnecessary medical procedures and denied treatment even after a safe and effective treatment is approved in the 1940s.

1938

The U.S. Congress passes a law that requires drugs to be proven safe before they are marketed to the public; this leads to the need for human drug trials.

1947

The Nuremberg Code, put forth by Allied nations at the end of World War II, creates a list of ten principles for researchers to follow when conducting clinical research.

1948

The United Nations adopts the first Universal Declaration of Human Rights as a response to Nazi atrocities revealed at the end of World War II; the declaration sets a standard by which the human rights activities of all nations are to be measured.

1949

The World Medical Association adopts an International Code of Medical Ethics and the Declaration of Geneva as the standard ethical codes for all the world's physicians to follow.

1956

The Willowbrook Hepatitis Study in Staten Island, New York, begin; his unethical study deliberately infects mentally ill children with a mild form of hepatitis in order to learn about the natural history of the disease.

1960s

Physicians, philosophers, and other academics begin to hold conferences on ethical issues in medicine.

1960

A new medical advance in dialysis allows effective removal of the body's waste products that are not filtered by damaged kidneys; Within two years, the sole kidney center offering the effective dialysis is flooded with patients needing treatment.

1962

An article in *Life* magazine called "They Decide Who Lives, Who Dies" describes the process a committee used to determine who qualified to receive lifesaving dialysis treatments; the shock over the knowledge that people could live or die based on the judgment of a committee stimulates academic debate by philosophers, historians, and theologians.

1964

The Declaration of Helsinki, written by physicians of the World Medical Association, offers recommendations for ethical conduct in experiments with humans; it is a reinterpretation of the Nuremberg Code focused on medical research.

1966

Dr. Henry K. Beecher writes an article describing twenty-two examples of research studies with controversial ethics that had been conducted by reputable researchers and published in major journals; this article heightens the awareness of unethical human research.

1969–1971

Ethics centers such as the Hastings Center (1969) and the Kennedy Institute (1971) are founded to formally address biomedical ethic issues.

1970s

The Joint Commission on Accreditation of Healthcare Organizations begins defining patients' rights and standards for organizational ethics at hospitals.

1971

The San Antonio Contraception study begins in San Antonio, Texas; a number of Mexican American women unknowingly participate in a study in which some of the women were given placebo pills instead of the oral contraceptives they requested.

1972

The American Hospital Association creates the Patient's Bill of Rights to strengthen consumer confidence in medical care, reaffirm the importance of a strong relationship between patients and their health-care providers, and emphasize the critical role consumers play in safeguarding their own health.

1974

Bioethics is made a subject heading by the Library of Congress; the U.S. Congress establishes the National Commission for the Protection of Human Subjects to identify the basic ethical principles that underlie the conduct of human research trials.

1975

The World Medical Association adopts the Declaration of Tokyo, a set of guidelines for physicians concerning torture and other cruel, inhuman, or degrading treatment in relation to detention and imprisonment.

1978–1979

The National Commission for the Protection of Human Subjects of Biomedical and Behavior Research issues the Belmont Report, which outlines ethical principles for the protection of human subjects in research.

1980–1983

The U.S. Congress creates the President's Commission for the Study of Ethical Problems in Medicine and Biomedical and Behavioral Research to examine biomedical ethics issues.

1981

The U.S. Department of Health and Human Services passes Title 45, Code of Federal Regulations, Part 46: Protection of Human Subjects; this regulation mandates certain protections for human subjects and sets parameters for human research.

1994

The American Medical Association drafts the Patient Protection Act; elements of the act are included in every health-system reform bill in both the House and Senate.

1995

An executive order creates the U.S. National Bioethics Advisory Commission.

1996

Prompted by public concern over medical errors, hospitals and others in Massachusetts form a Coalition for the Prevention of Medical Errors; the AMA and the American Hospital Association begin talking more openly about medical mistakes; the AMA also sets up a National Patient Safety Foundation, which funds research on error prevention; the U.S. Congress enacts the Health Insurance Portability and Accountability Act, which guarantees health-care plan eligibility for people who change jobs (if the new employer offers group insurance) and includes standards to protect the privacy of an individual's health information; in Scotland, Dr. Ian Wilmut and his team are the first to clone a sheep from adult cells; the cloned lamb is named Dolly.

1997

President William Clinton apologizes for the Tuskegee experiments.

1999

The Institute of Medicine releases *To Err Is Human*, a report that asserts forty-eight thousand to ninety-eight thousand Americans die in hospitals every year due to preventable medical errors; several state medical associations accuse managed health maintenance organizations of conspiring to withhold medical care and failing to tell patients of incentives to doctors to limit care; patients subsequently charge that they had received lower-quality care as a result.

2000

The National Institutes of Health issues guidelines that allow federal funding of embryonic stem-cell research.

2001

The Joint Commission on Accreditation of Healthcare Organizations begins requiring hospitals to notify patients if they are harmed by a medical error; President George W. Bush establishes the President's Council on Bioethics, which is charged with advising the president on bioethical issues that may emerge as a consequence of advances in biomedical science and technology; Bush announces his decision to limit federal funding of embryonic stem-cell research to the lines of embryonic stem cells in existence at that date.

2004

South Korean scientists headed by Dr. Hwang Woo Suk announce the world's first successfully cloned human embryo; unlike other past cloning claims, the scientists report their work in a prestigious, peer-reviewed journal, *Science*; the embryos were cloned not for reproductive purposes but as a source of stem cells.

2005

The U.S. House of Representatives passes a bill that would ease Bush's restrictions on federal funding for stem-cell research; a version of the bill passed in the House is introduced in the Senate; Suk admits that there are serious errors in his 2005 paper in *Science* and asks the journal to retract it; in addition, the Seoul National University investigation concludes all of the data were fabricated in the papers that Hwang's team published in *Science*; the U.S. Congress begins debate on the Patient Protection Act of 2005; the bill outlines basic standards for access to medical care, including requiring managed-care organizations to allow patients access to clinical trials and pay for the associated costs of the trials.

Organizations to Contact

American Medical Association (AMA)
515 N. State St., Chicago, IL   60610
(800) 621-8335
Web site: www.ama-assn.org

The AMA is the United States' largest professional organization for medical doctors. It helps set standards for medical practices and is a powerful lobby for physicians' interests. In order to address tough issues in medical ethics, the AMA includes an Institute for Ethics that establishes ethics policies to guide practicing physicians. It also develops educational programs that inform physicians on the means to address ethical and professional challenges. The association publishes several journals, including the monthly *Archives of Surgery* and the weekly *JAMA*.

American Society of Law, Medicine, and Ethics (ASLME)
765 Commonwealth Ave., Suite 1634, Boston, MA   02215
(617) 262-4990 • fax: (617) 437-7596
e-mail: info@aslme.org
Web site: www.aslme.org

The ASLME works to provide high-quality scholarship, debate, and critical thought to professionals concerned with ethical, legal, and social implications of health-care dilemmas. It publishes the *Journal of Law, Medicine and Ethics* and a quarterly newsletter.

Canadian Bioethics Society
561 Rocky Ridge Bay NW, Calgary, AL
  T3G 4E7 Canada
(403) 208-8027

e-mail: lmriddell@shaw.ca
Web site: www.bioethics.ca

The Canadian Bioethics Society is an organization of both individuals and organizations from a wide variety of fields, including medicine, law, theology, philosophy, and public health, sharing common interests in ethical debates and in the human dimensions of health research and practice. The society publishes a twice-yearly newsletter.

Center for Bioethics
University of Pennsylvania, Philadelphia, PA   19104
(215) 898-7136 • fax: (215) 573-3036
Web site: www.bioethics.upenn.edu

The Center for Bioethics at the University of Pennsylvania runs the largest bioethics Web site and focuses on the ethical, efficient, and compassionate practice of the life sciences and medicine. The center publishes a newsletter, *PennBioethics*, twice each year.

Center for Bioethics and Human Dignity (CBHD)
2065 Half Day Rd., Bannockburn, IL   60015
(847) 317-8180 • fax: (847) 317-8101
e-mail: info@cbhd.org
Web site: www.cbhd.org

The CBHD is a nonprofit group that promotes a Christian perspective on biomedical ethics issues. It helps individuals and organizations address pressing bioethical challenges, including managed care, end-of-life treatment, genetic intervention, euthanasia and suicide, and reproductive technologies. It is a national and international leader in producing a wide range of live, recorded, and written resources examining bioethical issues. Many of its articles are available on its Web site.

Center for Responsible Genetics (CRG)
5 Upland Rd., Suite 3, Cambridge, MA   02140
(617) 868-0870 • fax: (617) 491-5344

e-mail: crg@gene-watch.org
Web site: www.gene-watch.org

The CRG is a nonprofit group whose goal is to foster public debate about the social, ethical, and environmental implications of genetic technologies. CRG works through the media and concerned citizens to distribute accurate information and represent the public interest on emerging issues in biotechnology. CRG also publishes a bimonthly magazine, *GeneWatch*.

Centers for Disease Control and Prevention (CDC)
Division of Reproductive Health, Atlanta, GA   30341-3717
(770) 488-5200
Web site: www.cdc.gov/reproductivehealth

The CDC's Division of Reproductive Health provides informational reports on reproductive technologies; supports national and state-based surveillance systems to monitor trends and investigate health issues; conducts epidemiologic, behavioral, demographic, and health-services research; and works with partners to translate research findings into health-care practice, public-health policy, and health-promotion strategies. The division provides all of its reports free of charge directly through its Web site.

The Christian Medical Fellowship (CMF)
Partnership House, 157 Waterloo Rd., London   SE1 8XN
   United Kingdom
+44 (0)20 7928 4694 • fax: +44 (0)20 7620 2453
Web site: www.cmf.org.uk

The CMF is an organization that provides a Christian perspective on biomedical ethics issues. The CMF works to support Christian doctors, medical students, and other health-care professionals. It publishes numerous journals and articles on biomedical issues.

Euthanasia Research and Guidance Organization (ERGO)
24289 Norris Lane, Junction City, OR   97448-9559

(541) 998-1873
e-mail: ergo@efn.org
Web site: www.finalexit.org

The ERGO is a nonprofit educational corporation that believes voluntary euthanasia, physician-assisted suicide, assisted suicide, and self-deliverance are all appropriate life endings depending on the individual medical and ethical circumstances. The organization was founded in 1993, and its stated goal is to improve the quality of background research of assisted dying for persons who are terminally or hopelessly ill and wish to end their suffering. ERGO develops and publishes guidelines about life-ending decisions and offers many articles and books for purchase on their Web site.

The Hastings Center
21 Malcolm Gordon Rd., Garrison, NY   10524-4125
(845) 424-4040 • fax: (845) 424-4545
e-mail: mail@thehastingscenter.org
Web site: www.thehastingscenter.org

The Hastings Center is an independent, nonpartisan, and nonprofit bioethics research institute that is devoted to exploring the medical, ethical, and social implications of advances in health care, biotechnology, and the environment. Its publications include the *Hastings Center Report*.

Kennedy Institute of Ethics
Healy, 4th Floor, Georgetown University
Washington, DC   20057
(202) 687-8099 • fax: (202) 687-8089
Web site: kennedyinstitute.georgetown.edu

The Kennedy Institute of Ethics supports medical ethics research on a variety of topics. It supplies the National Library of Medicine with an online bioethics database and publishes reports and articles on many medical ethics topics.

President's Council on Bioethics
1801 Pennsylvania Ave. NW, Suite 700
Washington, DC   20006
(202) 296-4669
e-mail: info@bioethics.gov
Web site: www.bioethics.gov

Since 2001, the President's Council on Bioethics has had the role of advising the president on bioethical issues that may emerge as a consequence of advances in biomedical science and technology. Publications by the council include *Reproduction and Responsibility* and *Human Cloning and Human Dignity*.

Treuman Katz Center for Pediatric Bioethics
4800 Sand Point Way NE, PO Box 5371/71-1
Seattle, WA   98105
(206) 987-2000
e-mail: pcrc@seattlechildrens.org
Web site: research.seattlechildrens.org/centers/pediatric
-bioethics-center.asp

The Treuman Katz Center for Pediatric Bioethics is the nation's first bioethics center focused solely on pediatric issues. The center's goal is to create a permanent forum for national debate on the ethical issues that pediatric providers and researchers face each day. In order to educate health-care professionals and foster debate, the center holds annual pediatric bioethics conferences.

For Further Research

Books

Tom L. Beauchamp and LeRoy Walter, eds., *Contemporary Issues in Bioethics*. 5th ed. Belmont, CA: International Thomson, 1994.

Edwin Black, *War Against the Weak: Eugenics and America's Campaign to Create a Master Race*. New York: Four Walls Eight Windows, 2003.

Lesley Brown, *Our Miracle Called Louise: A Parent's Story*. New York: Grosset & Dunlap, 1984.

Chester R. Burns, ed., *Legacies in Ethics and Medicine*. New York: Science History, 1977.

David Cundiff, *Euthanasia Is Not the Answer*. Totowa, NJ: Humana, 1992.

Ian Dowbiggin, *A Merciful Life: The Euthanasia Movement in Modern America*. New York: Oxford University Press, 2003.

Peter G. Filene, *A Culture History of the Right-to-Die in America*. Chicago: Ivan R. Dee, 1998.

Kathleen Foley and Herbert Hendin, eds., *The Case Against Assisted Suicide: For the Right to End-of-Life Care*. Baltimore: Johns Hopkins University Press, 2002.

Francis Galton, *Essays in Eugenics*. London: Eugenics Society, 1909.

Derek Humphry, *Dying with Dignity: Understanding Euthanasia*. New York: Carol, 1992.

——, *Final Exit: The Practicalities of Self-Deliverance and Assisted Suicide for the Dying*. New York: Dell, 1996.

Derek Humphry and Mary Clement, *Freedom to Die*. New York: St. Martin's, 1998.

Albert Jonsen, *The New Medicine and the Old Ethics*. Cambridge, MA: Harvard University Press, 1990.

————, *"O Brave New World": Rationality in Reproduction*. New York: Cambridge University Press, 1996.

Leon R. Kass and James Q. Wilson, *The Ethics of Human Cloning*. Washington, DC: AEI, 1998.

Arlene Judith Klotzko, *A Clone of Your Own?* New York: Oxford University Press, 2004.

Shai J. Lavi, *The Modern Art of Dying: A History of Euthanasia in the United States*. Princeton, NJ: Princeton University Press, 2005.

Gregory Pence, *Classic Works in Medical Ethics*. Boston: McGraw-Hill, 1998.

————, *Who's Afraid of Human Cloning?* Lanham, MD: Rowman & Littlefield, 1998.

Thomas Percival, *Medical Ethics or a Code of Institutes and Precepts Adapted to the Professional Conduct of Physicians and Surgeons*. Manchester, UK: S. Russell, 1803.

Robert M. Veatch, *Cross Cultural Perspectives in Medical Ethics: Readings*. 2nd ed. Boston: Jones & Bartlett, 2000.

Periodicals

Marcia Angell, "No One Trusts the Dying," *Washington Post*, July 7, 1997.

Ronald Bailey and Dinesh D'Souza, "Our Biotech Future," *National Review*, March 5, 2001.

Thomas Bowden, "Assisted Suicide: A Moral Right," *Capitalism*, January 31, 2006.

Nell Boyce, "Could a Copy Improve on the Original?" *U.S. News & World Report*, January 13, 2003.

Geoffrey Cowley and Karen Springen, "Risk-Free Babies," *Newsweek*, March 11, 2002.

Alex Epstein, "To Ban Cloning Would Be a Moral Abomination," *Capitalism*, February 17, 2004.

Andrew Fergusson, "Why We Shouldn't Legalise Euthanasia," *Nucleus*, April 2005.

Richard M. Gula, "Dying Well: A Challenge to Christian Compassion," *Christian Century*, May 5, 1999.

Bernadine Healey, "A Humanoid in the Manger," *U.S. News & World Report*, December 23, 2002.

Daniel J. Kevles, "Eugenics and Human Rights," *British Medical Journal*, August 14, 1999.

Michael D. Lemonick et al., "The Rise and Fall of the Cloning King," *Time*, January 9, 2006.

Laurence McCullough, "Enlightenment Biomedical Ethics," *Kennedy Institute of Ethics Journal*, 1996.

C. Ben Mitchell, "Hurtling Toward Eugenics . . . Again," *Ethics & Medicine*, Summer 2002.

Matthew Nisbet, "Attack of the Metaphor," *American Prospect Online*, May 15, 2002.

Alex Salkever, "Building a Better Brain?" *Christian Science Monitor*, September 2, 1999.

James D. Watson, "Moving Toward the Clonal Man," *Atlantic*, May 1971.

Index